Mummy's Little Angels

Mummy's Little Angels

A mother's agonising story
of losing her sons to a
murderous father

DENISE WILLIAMS

with Julie McCaffrey

EBURY
PRESS

1 3 5 7 9 10 8 6 4 2

Ebury Press, an imprint of Ebury Publishing,
20 Vauxhall Bridge Road,
London SW1V 2SA

Ebury Press is part of the Penguin Random House group of companies
whose addresses can be found at global.penguinrandomhouse.com

Penguin
Random House
UK

This edition published by Ebury Press in 2015

www.eburypublishing.co.uk

A CIP catalogue record for this book is available from the British Library

ISBN 9780091958572

Printed and bound by CPI Group (UK) Ltd, Croydon CR0 4YY

MIX
Paper from
responsible sources
FSC® C018179

Penguin Random House is committed to a sustainable future
for our business, our readers and our planet. This book is made
from Forest Stewardship Council® certified paper.

In memory of Bret and Brad Lee.
I hope this in some way explains why Mummy is sorry.
We tried so hard to be happy.
We almost made it. xx

Contents

Prologue

The gifts are wrapped and laid out on the sofa. A football top with 'Owen' printed on the back, new pyjamas and a Nintendo game.

I know Owen will like the computer game most. It is much wanted and carefully vetted. I won't, I *can't*, have any violence in my home. No films with fighting, no games with the all-too-real shouts of conflict and pain.

The house is quiet, the children are asleep and the packed lunch and shoe-polishing chores are done to ease tomorrow's school-run stress. So in silence I relive the day he was born. I think most mums do this on their children's birthdays. Most won't have bittersweet memories like mine.

I remember the first few hours after Owen's birth so vividly. Gazing at my tiny baby boy in my arms, stroking his air-soft cheeks, kissing his dandelion-clock hair and thinking of both times I did exactly the same thing in the same maternity ward.

I was thrilled with the miracle of his new life, yet fearful of its fragility. I was overwhelmed with the mother's instinct to protect, yet mourned for the boys I could not. I was full of hope for my newborn's future but my own life was on pause while the court case loomed.

Tomorrow Owen will be 12 – my eldest child but not my first. The two big brothers he never knew smile shyly from frames on the wall above the sofa. Matching pale-blue polo shirts emphasise the striking similarities in their looks. Even their hair is parted the same way. Maybe only I'd notice that Bret has tomato-sauce stains around his mouth, which was the reason I decided not to buy the school portraits that year. Their headteacher was kind enough to send me the picture anyway. Afterwards.

So I sit in stillness before the morning's birthday fun and fuss. And I realise I don't know how to be a mum to a 12-year-old. I have no idea what challenges Owen will face over the next year, no clue what he'll like or learn.

I've never had a child who lived this long.

On my way to bed I look in on Owen and his little sisters, Katie and Grace, as they sleep. So peaceful, so beautiful. Safe.

And again I imagine I am back there in the old house at Linden Avenue checking on Bret and Brad Lee in the night. Their two beds side-by-side, together in sleep as they were every day. Brothers born 10 months apart who shared the same class at school, similar interests, a wide circle of friends and looks that meant they were mistaken for twins.

Again we are together; the three of us snuggled up in one single bed. Whenever their dad was out, usually getting drunk over a few games of snooker, my boys and I had 'duvet movie' nights. We wrapped Brad Lee's Batman duvet around us and watched the Disney film *Bambi* on their very own DVD player, which made them the envy of their friends. When Bambi's mother was killed, I made sure I was cuddling my boys close.

I knew Bret would be the first to cry. My happy-go-lucky little baby had grown more sensitive every year. Although older and an inch taller than his brother, he wasn't as tough as Brad Lee. When Brad Lee fell and cut his head on a Lego brick, it was Bret who cried at the sight of blood while his brother simply shrugged and carried on playing.

'It's so sad, Mummy,' Bret sobbed, burying his face into my chest. 'Who's going to look after Bambi now?'

'It's just a film, silly billy,' I soothed. 'Don't cry, darling.'

'But what if you died, too, Mummy?' he asked.

'I'm not going anywhere,' I said, kissing then ruffling his dark wavy hair. 'It's my job to look after you two every single day, every single hour until you're big, grown-up men. I love you too much to leave you.'

Brad Lee stretched his arms around me and his big brother and gave us both a squeeze.

'We love you, we do, Mummy,' said Brad Lee. 'We're best friends forever and ever, aren't we?'

'Yep – best friends forever,' I smiled.

And, as always on duvet movie nights, we three were so comfy in our three-way hug that we fell asleep in that tiny bed. I wish I could sleep as soundly these days.

Chapter 1
He Was No Angel

I was seven when I found out the man I called Dad was not my father. And I was glad about that.

Dave Angel had been with Mum since I was six months old and was the only father figure I'd known. Mum split from my real dad before I was born.

People must have thought Dave was such a good bloke to take on my mum, such a decent fella. Because, as well as having me, Mum already had two other little girls with her first husband: Angie was eight and Nicky was five when Dave moved in with Mum.

Money was so tight that we three girls slept in one big bed in a tiny maisonette at Tipton in Sandwell, West Bromwich. When we moved three miles away into a council house at Greets Green, we thought it was a palace because it had three bedrooms and a garden.

We needed the space because Mum was having a baby with Dave. Sarah is seven years younger than me and Amy was born three years later in 1986.

Until my younger sisters were born, I thought being beaten by Dave was the norm. Getting belted by a grown man for using too much washing-up liquid to do the dishes happened to most five-year-olds who liked bubbles, surely? Being booted in the shins was usual for any child who forgot to take their shoes off in the house, wasn't it?

With Sarah and Amy's arrival came a sense of life's injustices. Because I realised that Dave never punished his own two kids. Yet when it came to me and my big sisters, he inflicted extreme sanctions for minor misdemeanours. His level of ferocity grew as we did.

By the time we were teenagers Dave's favourite punishment was making us stand against a wall, holding two house bricks above our head for hours. If our arms tired and lowered, he'd belt us.

'Can I put the bricks down now? Please, I need a wee.'

'No way! You will stand there until I say so.'

Sometimes I wet myself because I had no choice. Then I'd be made to stand even longer in my urine.

When the ladder smashed through the front window I told Dave it was me, even though it was Nicky. Dave whacked me so hard with the buckle end of his belt across my back, legs and backside that I couldn't walk for days and had to take time off school. Taking the punishment didn't hurt as much as seeing and hearing my big sisters get a strapping. I couldn't bear to hear them scream and beg for Dave to stop. And I knew Nicky would be in for a severe lashing this time but she shouldn't have had to wash the outside of the windows, aged only 10.

Sometimes Dave left us alone. When he and Mum fancied an evening at the pub, we were abandoned for four or five hours at a time. Dave sent us to our rooms and placed tiny pieces of paper, strips of Sellotape or even hairs in the door hinges.

'If you DARE open that door I'll know because these papers will come out. God help you, I'll pulverise you!'

Sometimes we'd swear a draught must have blown the scraps of paper or hair from the gap between the door and its frame. We didn't open the door, honestly. But Dave didn't care. He gave us a kicking anyway.

'Come here, you little shit,' he said, loosening his belt and tearing it from his trouser loops so swiftly it made a whoosh sound.

'What have I told you?' Whip. 'About leaving the room when I tell you to stay in?'

Whip.

'When I tell you to do something...' Whip. 'YOU FUCKING WELL DO IT!'

Whip. Whip. Whip.

Mum's screams topped ours. 'Dave, enough! Stop! Jesus, Dave, they are just little girls.'

'Shurrup, woman!' he retorted. And Mum did quieten.

It's amazing how a punch in the mouth does that, incredible how a small woman can fly across the room with a fist in the face.

I'd never known Dave to have paid employment. He had been a roofer with his own business but it had gone bust. The only money he made came from fishing competitions and it took years for me to realise that his income was high. He once paid £1,000 for a fishing rod. The money was there, but it was spent on angling and drinking.

There was no need for us kids to be such little tramps. Our clothes were hand-me-downs from neighbours and friends. One Christmas our toys came from the Samaritans because one of the teachers at school worked for the charity and used to call Mum every Christmas to ask if we needed help. Treats were a packet of Refreshers or Chewits, the cheapest sweets you could get. And we'd have to earn them by spending a whole weekend doing backbreaking work on our knees, picking stones and weeds from the garden. If my big sisters and I ever picked a plant rather than a weed or even whispered to each other while working, we'd get a crack over the head with a shovel.

Beatings from my stepdad were dished out far more than sweets.

Except if you were one of *his* kids. Nicky, Angie and I would do the arduous work in the vegetable patch while Sarah and Amy sat cosily inside, watching telly and eating the sweets they hadn't earned.

At first we were thrilled to have two little sisters – pretty little real-life dollies to play with. But then we had to look after them and do all the donkey work: changing nappies, washing clothes, preparing their meals. We started to resent that all Mum and Dave's attention went on them. Angie, Nicky and I felt shut out on our own when they came along.

Not that we had much time to dwell. We three were young slaves, constantly doing chores and serving the others in the household with Dave as our cruel master.

'Don't even think about not doing your jobs properly or you'll get what's coming to you!'

Whenever he came home from spending hours with his fishing mates, Dave would run his finger across the top of the door frame or the curtain pole. If there was a speck of dust you were in for a good hiding.

He gave us 10 minutes to get back from school, which was at least a 20-minute walk. The instant the bell rang I changed into my trainers and ran all the way home. Walking back with a classmate was out of the question. Taking a friend home to play or for tea was an impossibility.

Once home we'd obediently hang up our coats and schoolbags before starting to vacuum, polish, weed the garden, help make tea and then we'd wash up afterwards. Homework was done but it was rushed. Because in the evening we'd have to sit on the living-room floor beside Dave on his chair to scratch his back, squeeze his spots, scrub the hard skin off his feet and clean his toenails. Mum was always nearby doing chores but never objected. Dave treating us that way was just part of life, part of our daily routine.

'You're useless at doing me feet,' Dave would sneer at me in disgust, kicking me out of his way. 'Go on, get to bed!'

We willed it to be bedtime.

Our bedroom had two bunks and a single bed, greying woodchip wallpaper, a threadbare brown carpet and an ugly chest of drawers. Yet my sisters and I loved being sent there at night. Once there, away from Dave, we could whisper about our shared ultimate dream. It wasn't to own a pony, be a princess or go to Disneyland. All we really wanted, all we fantasised about, was leaving home.

'Our real dad would never treat us like Dave does,' Angie said to Nicky. 'And your real dad was nice when he was with Mum, you know, Dee?'

Thinking of my real dad was my secret hobby, my favourite escape.

My real dad would go mental if he knew what Dave was doing to me. He would pull up outside the house in a shiny car, hammer on the door and demand to know why on earth Dave thought he could treat his daughter so badly. He'd smack Dave in the face and, as he fell to the floor, Dad would lift me into his strong arms and rescue me from the house of misery.

He'd apologise for ever leaving me and would drive me to his house, which had a big dinner in the oven, a full fridge, hot radiators and a bedroom just for me. In my room at my real dad's house I could do homework quietly, welcome school friends to stay the night and sleep peacefully without the sound of Dave hurling Mum against the wall. I'd feel welcome there. Wanted. Safe.

My real dad would say: 'I just want you to be happy, Denise. We've lost so many years apart so we have to make up for them. Make yourself comfortable in my home, because you're the most important person in my life. Let me help you with your homework then have a big chat about all the things you like in life. At the weekend let's go shopping together for some decent clothes instead of those rags.'

But that was just a daydream. It would never happen, said my mum. My real dad was, by her account, a waster, a troublemaker and no good to anyone: 'a real bastard'.

I remember seeing him only once. At my auntie's anniversary party, when the kids were kept in the kitchen while the grown-ups took over the rest of the house.

Being the cheeky girl I was, I wandered into the living room to see if there were any tomatoes in the adults' room. A really big man with very curly black hair was sitting in a chair and he bent down to speak to me.

'Hello, babe, how are you? Are you all right?'

'Yes, thank you.'

He pressed a pound note into my hand. I'd never held one before. Keen to show it off, I darted back to the kids in the kitchen.

'That's a lot of money. Where did you get that?' asked my cousin Julie.

'From that bloke there,' I said, pointing to the man, who was still smiling at me.

'You know who that is, don't you? That's your real dad.'

Now that was a bombshell. The first I knew that Dave wasn't really my dad. And in that moment of realisation there was no sadness. No sense of betrayal or loss, just excitement: I had a new dad.

Ecstatic, I ran to my mum. 'That's my real dad over there, Mum! Do you see him? Look, I've got a new daddy!'

But Mum's face fell – she knew what was coming.

Dave heard the fuss and stormed off, leaving Mum and me to walk seven miles home.

That night Dave battered my mum and I got sent to bed. I didn't mention my real dad to them after that.

Angie and Nicky still saw their real dad, Ray. Angie ran away to be with him twice. She was 16 the first time and had just started working but, when she turned up to do her day's shift as a power press operator at the spring factory in Oldbury Road, Dave stormed into the factory and pulled her home by the hair. Half her hair was ripped out.

Her colleagues were too scared of Dave to intervene. When Angie went back to work they urged her to call the police. But she never did.

A few months later she took off to stay with Ray again because she heard he had cancer. He died soon afterwards. Of course Dave was full of the sympathy and softness you'd expect from him at such a sad time.

'It's your fault your dad died. All that stress of you suddenly turning up and demanding to live with him sped up the cancer. You killed him, Angie, you did. You should be ashamed.'

Even though there really was nothing about fat, bald, ugly, violent Dave that was nice, a weird sense of family loyalty meant I also kept quiet about my hellish home life.

I didn't have many friends at school. I'd like to think it was just because I wore glasses and was called four-eyes, but it was probably because my big sisters and me were the poorest and worst-dressed kids at school. Every year Mum got vouchers to spend on our uniforms at Oakes school shop in Oldbury but they only sold long, pleated skirts. So, while our friends had cute little above-the-knee skirts and dainty ankle socks, we were the three old grannies in long skirts and knee socks. Even though we hated our uniforms, they were immaculate. Dave made us neatly fold our pile of clothes each night and, if they weren't perfect, he'd chuck the lot on the ground so we'd have to fold them all again.

Lisa, my really good school friend, was the only one I confided in. She was from a warm and loving family and her eyes widened saucer-size when I told her about Dave stamping on my mum's chest or having to take down my jeans so he could belt me.

She asked me, 'Why don't you tell the police? Why don't you run away and come to my house?'

But I was too scared to flee. Especially after seeing what had happened to Angie.

Lisa loyally never told anyone else about my bullying stepdad. None of the teachers or any other adults knew about my brutal upbringing. No one intervened. They must have seen the bruises, black eyes, swollen lips, noticed the limp. Must have noted the absences. But it was different then: everyone was too scared to make accusations and I never reported anything.

Maybe they suspected but they just didn't know what to do. Maybe there was nothing they could do. After any absences from school, which were all because of Dave's beatings, teachers would quietly ask, 'Is everything OK at home?' I always insisted all was fine. So what could the teachers do? They couldn't ask me to undress to check out my cuts and belt marks. I was a prefect and a good girl at school so there was no reason to call for meetings with my parents. Only one teacher got an insight into my home life, quite by accident.

On the way to school, when I was around 13, I was run over by a car. I was halfway over a pedestrian crossing when a stolen car zoomed through the red light, knocked me down and drove over my left leg. I was bleeding and had a tyre imprint on my leg. But because I was terrified I'd get blamed or into bother, I got straight back up and half walked, half hopped all the way to school.

A teacher who'd been in traffic saw everything and tracked me down at school. He was so nice because he said he was concerned I would be in a lot of pain. But when he insisted I went home, I felt scared.

'Honestly, Sir, I'm fine. I don't want to go home – I'll be in trouble.'

'Don't be so silly – why will you be in trouble? Come on, I'm taking you home now and you will *not* be in trouble.'

At the house Dave looked furious as soon as he saw me on the doorstep with a teacher.

'What has she done now?'

The teacher explained that he'd seen me in a road accident and thought I was in too much pain to be at school. Dave was his understanding self.

'Must've been her fault. Dee must have been messing around to have been clipped by a car.'

The teacher looked pretty pissed off then. 'No, she wasn't doing anything wrong at all. She's been really hurt and really brave.'

To be honest, I was in agony but I'd never have dared admit that to Dave. Just like I refused to cry when he walloped me because he would have loved that. Over the next few days when I was off school he enjoyed seeing me struggle to walk around the house as I worked through his extra-long list of chores.

Probably every kid thinks they get punished more than their siblings. And I'm no different. I always felt like the black sheep of the family, I even looked like one. I have raven-coloured hair and dark features while my four sisters have blonde or mousey brown hair and fair colouring. I stood out. And Dave liked striking me down more than anyone.

Having a different dad to the rest seemed the root of Dave's detestation of me. I'd heard that Mum was still with my dad, called Dennis Paige, when she started dating Dave. Apparently Dave hated Dennis with a passion and I'm convinced he took that out on me.

Despite all the vicious attacks she endured, the humiliation he heaped upon her, Mum never told us she wanted to leave Dave. But when he went on his annual fishing trip to Denmark I could tell she was happy. She had time for us during that week and we'd all sit on the front-room floor playing cards. We were close when Dave wasn't around. But before he came home we'd see Mum's shutters come down again and she'd say, 'You'd better get on with all your chores before Dave gets back.'

We always said Mum was brainwashed by Dave.

Alcohol was a huge problem in their relationship. They both knew it but never did anything to stop it. When they'd had a drink, Mum got mouthy and Dave got busy with his fists. She'd answer back; he'd punch her.

'Think hitting a woman makes you a man, does it, Dave?'

Scream.

'That's right – give me a black eye to match my other one, will you?'

Whack.

Nicky, Angie and I begged Mum to be quiet so the beating would stop. Dave would roar at us, 'Do you want one as well?'

But we didn't urge her to leave Dave. God, no. She was so manipulated by him, so under his control, she would have told him and it would all have kicked off.

Instead, Mum took Dave's bashings for petty things like dropping a fag butt down the loo. She put up with his savage treatment of three of her five kids and depriving us in every way he could.

She never called the police; she never threw him out or ran away – she stayed with him because she was too fearful to leave.

I understand that now.

Chapter 2
'This Is The Life You Deserve'

The Oakdale working men's club wasn't known for playing the latest, coolest tunes. My sisters and I rolled our eyes at each other when the cheesy ballad 'Lady in Red' boomed from the speakers.

Mum and Dave's idea of spending time as a family was dragging us all here. While they knocked back lager, we kids sat there sulking and trying to make a glass of warm pop and bag of Salt 'n' Shake crisps last all night. The crisp packet was torn at three sides and laid out flat on the table in front so we could all share the one bag Dave allowed us. We constantly squabbled about who'd scoffed the most.

At 16, I was getting a taste of being an adult. I'd left school in July 1991 with nine GCSEs at B and C grades and started a course at Smethwick College to become a care-worker. I chose the course mainly because carers often got live-in jobs, which could mean fleeing home as soon as possible. I needed a ticket out and that course was my fastest route.

I was slim-built but the boys on the milk float wolf-whistled whenever they passed, so I suspected I might have curves in the right places. I even had a boyfriend, a sea cadet called Gary Roberts, before he'd sailed away for months. I wasn't a virgin anymore.

That night at the club, a much older man was walking slowly across the dance floor, smiling and pointing at me. As he got closer, he beckoned.

'Come on. Would you like this dance with me, lady in red? You *have* to dance with me. Just this song? You're wearing a red dress – you gotta dance with me. I won't hear no.'

I was wearing a fine-knit scarlet dress, which had bat-wing sleeves and a tight skirt. It was a hand-me-down from my cousin, and Angie and Nicky had both worn it many times. Our clothes were never exclusive.

Had Dave not glared, had Mum not thrown me a filthy look, I probably would have turned him down with a shake of my head until he sloped off. But I was grown up now and very headstrong: I would show them I could do what I liked.

I took his out-stretched hand and headed across the sticky carpet to the drink-strewn dance floor. While we swayed together he held me close, *too* close. I felt uncomfortable but knew that our slow dance would be driving Mum and Dave mad so the rebel in me didn't pull away. Mum walked out to the lounge in disgust, Dave looked horrified.

Until that moment we had never spoken but I knew who he was because he was the talk of the club. His name was Steve

Wilson and he was flash and argumentative – and, at 34, more than twice my age.

And he was keen. Mad keen.

Using the loud music as an excuse to talk close to my ear, so I could feel his breath and lips on my skin in a half kiss, Steve said, 'You are beautiful, do you know that? I saw you over there and thought you looked too good, too classy to be in here. And you also looked a bit miserable, sitting over there with your family. Why's someone as sexy as you looking so sad?'

I don't know if I had much in the way of witty repartee in those days. I don't know what I said back, if anything at all. I just remember Steve kept piling it on thick. His compliments were making me giddy.

'You smell nice. You look amazing. I need to see you again tomorrow – will you meet me? I'm well off, you know. I can pick you up in my car, take you somewhere nice, treat you like a lady, a princess. You're as pretty as a princess, do you know that?'

He was wearing a denim jacket, something few people I knew could afford. He had nice jeans and an open shirt that showed off a gold cross necklace hanging against his hairy chest. His dark curly hair reminded me of my real dad. And his attention, his body against mine, sent my hormones soaring. The chemistry was intoxicating.

When I sat back down with my family, Nicky gave me a sharp elbow in the ribs. Dave could not look at me. He and Mum hated Steve because they said he caused trouble wherever he went. They called him an arsehole when he raced up and down the streets in his car with his terrified young son and daughter in the back. And they couldn't stand his brash, show-off, shit-stirring ways.

But I didn't care. Our first date had been arranged.

I was glad Steve's four-wheel-drive car was distinctive with its silver roof and dark metallic green bodywork because when he turned up at college to pick me up I wanted everyone to see. A rich, older man with a car was here to date *me*.

I was thrilled when he pulled up near the college gates and giggled with my friends when he waved and winked at me.

'You jammy git,' they said. 'Look at his car!'

Desperately trying to appear as if I was mature enough for a man like him, I tried to ignore the screams of excitement in my head. I'd practised what I thought was a nonchalant smile, which I thought he'd find sexy. *Cosmo* mag always said women should try to appear aloof; mysterious, like. Friends said that, if you were too into a guy, blokes could sense desperation, like a dog sniffs fear, and they'd be off chasing someone else.

So, while Steve stared as I walked the hundred yards from the college grounds to his car, I tossed my long hair over my shoulders, half-smiled and tried to walk as seductively as I could. I hoped he'd like what he saw in me right then; I hoped everyone in the whole college saw me right then.

Had I not played such an act, I'd have beamed and bounded over to him like a hyperactive puppy.

'Hi, Princess,' he said, opening the car door.

It was a freezing January day but I was boiling. As soon as I got into his car a patch on the passenger side of the windscreen misted up and I was mortified that my nerves had shown themselves so obviously. But I couldn't help it. All my senses were heightened. I can remember the smooth, luxuriant feel of the grey and green-striped velour car seats. The smell of his musky aftershave, the sight of his four gleaming gold sovereign rings and two chunky diamond rings glinting in the sun as he drove through the countryside. The sound of his car engine, roaring as he raced up country lanes and around blind bends, frightened yet impressed me. And the taste of the Extra Strong mints I'd eaten all morning in anticipation of a kiss.

Most of the lads I knew hadn't learned to drive so owning a car was at least five years off for them – never mind a cracking car like this. Steve told me it was a Daihatsu Fourtrak and went on for a good while about horsepower, nought-to-sixty and all sorts of other reasons why it was so special. I understood none of the technical car-talk but was wowed by it all.

Lads my age would have considered taking me to McDonald's an extravagant treat. They thought snogging up against the bus shelter was a sexy and romantic seduction. To be honest, I did too back then. Since no one around me had a pound to spare, I was grateful if someone shared their bar of Twix with me. Eating a bag of chips with a lad while you sat on the wall in the park signified a meaningful relationship.

Going to the pictures with Gary to watch *My Girl* was the best date I ever had – the *only* date. Gary bought the tickets and, because I couldn't afford the expensive chocolates at the cinema kiosk, I bought sweets from Kwik Save and smuggled them into the cinema down the front of my jacket. We got the bus to West Bromwich town centre together and Gary's dad gave us a lift back. But when I got home Dave told me off for being late and I was punched in the head for daring to argue that I couldn't leave until the film had finished.

Now, with Steve, I was in a far higher league. He was so much older and, judging by his fancy clothes and big-man chat, he was rich. Here I was, in an expensive car, being driven to a country pub for lunch. I had never in my life been taken to a real restaurant.

'Pick whatever you like from the menu,' said Steve. 'It doesn't matter what it costs.'

I tried to look like I was entirely used to such treatment. I failed.

The menu said 'local pheasant'. So, trying to be posh, I asked the waitress, 'And just how local is the pheasant?' Steve nearly cried laughing at that.

Soon the conversation flowed. And so did the white wine. I had never touched a drop of alcohol until then and had never been tempted after seeing what drink had done to Mum and Dave. Steve ordered it and I didn't want to seem babyish by objecting that I'd never even sipped wine.

It made me light-headed, giggly and loosened my tongue, because, as soon as Steve asked how I got on with my stepdad, stories I'd kept secret about him being a brute poured out.

Steve responded by saying everything I didn't even know I wanted to hear.

'I'd love to take you away from all that. Love to steal you from your stepdad and call you mine. I've been watching you for a while. I want to look after you, mould you. You could move in with me, live as a kept woman. You'd never have to work, never need to do none of that studying at college. I'd put you on a pedestal and let no one hurt you, no one touch you, ever again.'

Steve definitely sounded smitten with me. He'd had a hard time with women lately, he said. His wife had died from cancer, leaving him with two kids and a broken heart because he had truly loved her. And, although he had joined a dating agency and met a few other women, they had been 'bad women'.

I was totally different, he said. An angel. He wanted me to be his next wife because he could feel intense attraction. He said he had a strong instinct to protect me and provide for me.

Everything he said dazzled me. Not just his gushing proclamations of how beautiful I was but his stories of his tough SAS training and top-secret missions around the world. He helped foreign governments rescue kidnap victims while armed with Kalashnikov guns. He was taught to kill a man with a single blow and mimed how to punch someone's nose upwards so the bone goes up into their brain and causes instant death. And he went on for ages about how cutting someone in the left carotid artery of the neck is the quickest way to kill.

He sounded like a living, breathing action man. A hero. Superhero. His life was an action film. I knew that if anyone could sort out Dave Angel, Steve could.

And if I was going to leave a life of poverty, Steve was there to lead the way. As one of the most highly trained SAS soldiers in the nation, going on short tours with the Special Forces would earn him 20 grand a time. He swore I'd never need to worry about money ever again – I just needed to stay home and look after his two kids while he went on his missions.

'Come 'ere. Don't sit opposite me, Princess. Sit here beside me – you're too far away and I want to give you a gift.'

As I sat alongside him, Steve gave me a tiny deep-red velvet-covered box. Inside was a beautiful ring with four little blue stones surrounded by white stones. I gasped. 'Wow!'

'Do you like it? It's nine-carat gold. And it's just for you.'

Steve slipped the ring on my engagement finger. I felt I was living a scene from *Pretty Woman*. No one had ever given me a present like that. The most expensive thing I'd ever owned was my school shoes.

I was so overwhelmed, and a little drunk, that I questioned whether it was really happening.

'Are you sure? This ring is really for me? It's too expensive I've never had anything like this. You should have it back.'

'No way, sweetheart! That ring is yours. What's mine is yours. And there's plenty more where that came from. This is the life you deserve.'

As Steve paid the bill with a pile of cash and left a tip on top, I'd like to say I thought about looking after him, helping to mend his grieving heart and raise his bereaved kids. But I didn't – I only thought about sorting my own life out.

We had undeniable chemistry. I fancied him rotten and there was a definite attraction there. I didn't really know what love was but I knew he was in love with me.

Three weeks later I moved in with him.

Chapter 3

'He's A Bad 'Un, I'm Telling You'

I secretly packed and just left. Mum was still in bed and Dave was out fishing, so Nicky tiptoed downstairs with me and helped carry my bags. Steve was waiting for me in his car, just out of sight down the street.

Amy and Sarah were having their breakfast. Saying goodbye to my little sisters was the only moment I felt sad.

'Ta-ra, sweethearts,' I said, kissing their cheeks and giving them an extra-tight hug. 'Have a great day at school and be good girls, won't you? See you later.'

As I walked out the back door I had to let them believe I was leaving for college, knowing full well I was leaving forever.

Angie had already moved out so Nicky was the only one I'd told. As she handed me my bags, she said, 'You're lucky, getting out of here. I really hope it works out for you but I'm worried for you, Dee. You know he has a really bad past, don't you?'

'I know, Nicky, but that's the past. He's changed, people change.'

I was mature enough to make my own judgements and felt sure I was making the right decision. In fact, I couldn't wait for Steve to put his foot down and drive me away.

I phoned Mum later.

'I've moved in with Steve Wilson. I'm not coming back,' I told her.

Mum was stunned. She hadn't even known I'd been seeing Steve.

First she tried a softly-softly lecturing approach to convince me to return.

'Listen, Dee. He treated his first wife really badly and will treat you the same. Come home, love. Come home and we'll say no more about it.'

When I wouldn't budge, she took a harder line.

'You're making a huge mistake. If you don't change your mind, don't think you can come back here. You've made your bed and you can lie in it. I'll have nothing to do with you if you're with that man. He's a bad 'un, I'm telling you. Don't come running to me when it all goes wrong.'

Dave took the phone. 'Why would you want to live with a total bastard like that?' he said.

The irony of that nearly made me laugh.

'If you're with him, you'll never be allowed under my roof again.'

I was adamant I would never go back. Mum and Dave washed their hands of me.

'I don't care. I'm 16 now, I can do what I want.'

I'd had enough of the volatile atmosphere, the violence, bullying, poverty and slavery. I was tired of the voices raised, doors slammed and curses sworn.

And Steve really wanted me to live with him. 'I can't wait for you to move in,' he'd told me. 'You'll be so happy with me, I'll make sure of it. You won't need a job or any of that college stuff. I'll look after you.'

That was the life I wanted, the escape I craved. Bypassing all the studying to get what I ultimately wanted was a dream. I felt lucky, wanted, admired. Loved, even.

When I arrived at Steve's two-up, two-down cottage at 20 Linden Avenue, Great Barr, my entire worldly belongings barely filled four carrier bags. A few cheap clothes, scuffed shoes, bits of make-up, dog-eared posters of Jon Bon Jovi. I was embarrassed I had so little.

But Steve was soothing and understanding. 'Don't worry, Dee. You don't need anything from your parents, you've got me now. You'll want for nothing. Here, try these on.'

He showed me dresses he'd bought for his wife, Trish, which still hung in her wardrobe. They were gorgeous and looked expensive. Some, he said, even cost £40, which was a lot then. They were the type of dresses that would cost £100 now.

I didn't mind wearing them because they were far more sophisticated than the cast-offs I was used to but I refused to try on her shoes. Pointy-toed, high-heeled and brightly coloured, one pair even had a gold bow on the side. They were for a much older woman and I didn't want them.

Over the next few days I started to find pictures of Trish and sympathy cards dated only a few months back. I thought she'd died years beforehand; I didn't know I was wearing another woman's dress that was almost still warm.

It was difficult to bring up the subject of Steve's late wife because he was really cut up about her passing. She was only 33 when she died and her death had been traumatic. Steve had told doctors at the hospital he wanted her to die at home, but, when they insisted that wasn't possible, he ripped out the drip tubes and carried Trish from the ward, barging through security.

Steve said Trish had died on the couch at home, but I wasn't to feel funny about sitting there because he'd bought a new one. He'd made me a new wardrobe so I could put my belongings there and Trish's things could be left just as they were, like a shrine.

Trish was everywhere in the house. On top of the telly was a picture of her and Steve on their wedding day with the church in the background. That picture was never to be touched. On Steve's bedside cabinet was a photo of Trish in her wedding dress, dead in her coffin. And on the top shelf in the other bedroom was a wooden box containing Trish's ashes.

Steve insisted she was even in the electricity supply. Whenever the lights flickered, he'd say, 'That's a sign from Trish. Hello, Trish, darling – you always said you would never leave me.'

Steve wanted me to act like Trish. He wanted me to look like Trish, to actually *be* Trish. It took only a few days of living with him to work that out. That's why he told me to wear her clothes. And that's why he tried to strip out the colour of my jet-black hair to dye it ash blonde, like hers.

Steve loved to comb my waist-length hair after my shower, and one day he started brushing and backcombing until it puffed right out – just like Trish's in the photos I'd found.

'You should do your hair like this,' he said.

Then he suggested I tried colouring it and produced a box of hair dye from the bathroom cabinet. He helped me slather on the strong-smelling mixture but after an hour of having pungent, stinging bleach on my hair it turned tangerine.

'I'm bloody ginger!' I cried, appalled to see my marmalade-coloured hair under the towel.

'It's OK, don't worry,' said Steve, hastily turning me away from the mirror and bending me over the sink to rinse the dye off. 'We can dye it black again.'

From then on, in his quest to make me look how he wanted me to, Steve opted for shopping rather than cloning. We went to high-street shops that were so expensive I'd never dared set foot in them before. He was so generous. If I liked a dress or a top, he'd buy it in five or six different colours.

And he really liked shopping with me. He loved helping me choose every little thing, right down to shoes, knickers, bras and tights. I loved that – I wanted him to like my clothes, to fancy me. If he didn't like something, then neither did I.

I never went shopping on my own; I never had money of my own. 'You don't need money, you have me,' Steve smiled. 'I'll just follow you, picking up the bills. You're like the Queen 'cos she never carries cash – you're *my* queen.'

I got a real rush from leaving shops weighed down with bags full of clothes. Even better was bumping into anyone from college when I was out shopping with Steve.

'Steve's bought me three new blouses today, you know,' I'd boast. I felt proud to be seen out with him, this much older, handsome man who was clearly loaded. This man could have had anyone but had picked me. I felt so grown up, like I'd really made it.

If my real dad could see me now, he'd be so proud that his little girl had grown up and landed such a nice man. Dennis would probably be great friends with Steve and we'd invite him for Sunday lunches so he could see that I now lived in a posh private house.

Steve's house used to be a farm labourer's cottage and, because it lay on an unadopted gravel road 20ft from the canal bank, it was quiet because no traffic passed by. From the front it looked like a little white house with ivy growing around the window but the house was much longer than it was wide and stretched right back. It had two big bedrooms upstairs and downstairs was a living room, kitchen and long hallway to the bathroom. Steve had built a cabin extension out the back, which had a terrace area, kitchen, bedroom and snooker room.

I knew friends who waved from the bus stop when I drove by in Steve's ace car were jealous. I knew my mates at college wished they didn't have to stick in and study for years just to get a low-paid, dead-end job when I was already enjoying all the trappings of a good life without the hard work.

They didn't exactly tell me that because I didn't see much of my friends once I moved in with Steve. He convinced me to jack in my course.

'You've got too much to do in the house. And what do you need all that swotting for, anyway? You don't need a career now I'm looking after you. Your swotty college friends won't understand that.'

Being spoiled made the hard things about living with Steve slightly easier. Because, as much as I liked showing off my luxurious, grown-up life to friends, things weren't perfect. My relationship with Steve's kids was difficult. Mainly because his son, Konrad, was only two years younger than me, and his daughter, Stacey, was four years my junior.

As soon as I moved into their home, I had a chat with Konrad and Stacey and explained that I didn't want to try to replace their mum. I felt really sorry for them. It must have been so hard to lose their mum then see someone only slightly older than them move into their home, sleep in their mum's bed and wear her clothes.

I hadn't met Konrad and Stacey until the day I moved in but I'd seen them before at the working men's club, sitting quietly with a bottle of pop while their dad played pool. We'd never spoken yet all of a sudden we were living together and expected to get on brilliantly.

And at first we did get on really well. We were friendly just like three kids, messing around and throwing cushions at each other in toy fights. But Steve didn't want that, didn't like the younger side of me. If ever we three were mucking about, he'd storm into the room with a face like thunder. Konrad and Stacey would immediately fall silent and sit up straight with their arms folded. He'd say to them, 'Don't you two think it's time you went to bed?' Then he'd turn to me. 'You are older than them, you've got a far more mature head on your shoulders. Start acting your age! You're supposed to be setting a good example to my kids.'

Steve wanted me to be more like a stepmum to his children and help keep them in line but that was so hard. At 16 I had pretty much brought my younger sisters up, but I couldn't baby Konrad because he was already taller than me. Stacey, at 12, was almost the same height. So, to hammer home the point that I was to be treated like an adult and they were kids, Steve encouraged me to drink alcohol. I hated the taste and the fact it made me feel so woozy I couldn't walk, couldn't think, couldn't speak. But I soon learned that refusing to drink with Steve made him furious.

'Trish would always have a beer with me. She loved drinking with me. She was great fun, was Trish,' he told me.

Late one night, after another fallout because I'd declined a bottle of beer, Steve bundled me into his car and sped to the cemetery. We had to climb over the gates to find Trish's grave in the dark.

'Hello, Trish, my darling. You always liked having a beer with me. Here's a beer. Cheers, my love.'

With that he poured a bottle of beer on to her grave. It gave me the creeps but I tried to understand that Steve was still raw with grief. I tried not to feel upset each time he told me I would never be the woman Trish was. It didn't feel good to know he preferred someone dead to me, but it was impossible to compete with a ghost.

Steve made it clear I could never come anywhere close to replacing Trish in his affections and told me his kids felt exactly the same. But I did my best. I tried to look after Konrad and Stacey as well as I could – making dinners, cleaning the house, washing and ironing their clothes – but emotionally I didn't understand what they needed from me.

Steve was very direct about exactly what *he* needed from me. He said the main thing that made him feel happy was making love. He made Konrad and Stacey get paper rounds so they'd have to go to bed early and be out of the house at the crack of dawn so we could be alone.

He and I spent a lot of time alone. In those early weeks we spent most of the day in bed together, only leaving the bedroom for food, drinks and showers. We had sex numerous times a day and through the night. Steve just could not get enough sex. It felt as if we were always at it. Although I wasn't a virgin, I was inexperienced. I never refused Steve sex because I assumed you had sex all the time when you moved in with someone, so it was just the way I had to be. And all the time, the picture of Trish wearing her wedding dress in her coffin was inches away from us.

Within a month of moving in, I'd realised that living with Steve's kids and their late mum was going to be way harder than I'd ever imagined. But by then I had other things on my mind, much bigger things. Because a pregnancy test said I would soon be a mum myself.

Chapter 4
The First Blow

When I told Steve I was expecting, he said, 'Is it mine?'

I'd been sick every morning for 10 days when Steve bought me a pregnancy test. He sat on the edge of the bath and insisted he watch as I peed on to the stick.

'Steve, give me some privacy,' I begged him. 'I don't want you here when I'm having a wee.'

'Dee, this could be an important moment in our lives. I wanna be right here with you.'

I'd moved in with him six weeks earlier. And now, according to the two blue lines on the plastic stick in my hand, there would be another little houseguest.

'Is it mine? I mean, it couldn't be your ex-boyfriend's baby?'

'It's definitely yours, Steve,' I said. 'The dates don't tally at all.'

Steve and I hadn't used a condom, nor even discussed contraception, so had been having unprotected sex. Every day.

I was elated. I loved my baby the instant I saw the test results and felt immediately maternal. In that moment I wasn't lonely anymore. The sense of never being on my own now I had a baby inside me was the most comforting, joyous, optimistic feeling I'd ever known.

My child would be the most loved in the world. My little one would want for nothing and would have none of the hardship I'd had. I would be the best, most adoring mum any kid could wish for. I really was grown up now.

Once the news sank in that he would be a daddy again, Steve was chuffed to bits.

'We'll have a boy – my little soldier,' he said.

There weren't many people I could call with my baby news. Mum wasn't speaking to me and I'd lost touch with my friends since quitting college. I didn't have a mobile phone and my sisters had stopped calling the house because Steve always told them I was too busy to talk. And I didn't know where my real dad was to tell him he'd be a granddad.

'Some family you've got,' said Steve. 'They don't care about you much if they don't even ring.'

Steve told the world. First, he sat Konrad and Stacey down and said, 'Dee's pregnant, so you'll be having a little brother or sister.' Neither said anything. They just looked at their dad, then me – and then the floor.

He bragged to all his mates down the club, 'You know I've got Dee up the duff, don't you? No wonder – at it like rabbits, we are. Insatiable!'

I think it made him feel macho. I think he liked that I needed him even more. I know it didn't dampen his need for sex. Even when my belly swelled so big that he had to buy me maternity tops and jeans, he was still constantly at me.

'I'm scared we'll squash the baby,' I said, trying to push him off.

'Don't be silly, the baby will be fine. You're not like Trish – she had sex right up until she gave birth.'

Steve made sure he came to every doctor's appointment. He said he had to be there. If anyone had raised eyebrows because of our glaringly obvious age gap or the fact we'd only recently started seeing each other, I wasn't aware of it.

I wouldn't have cared anyway. Being pregnant at 16 isn't on most teenagers' wish list; it certainly wasn't on mine. But now I was with child the world seemed a happier place. I felt really special, like I'd achieved something incredible. And I looked after myself better than I ever had. It felt like there was a Ready Brek glow around me – I was untouchable.

A scan showed we were having a boy – a perfectly healthy little fella.

Steve was overjoyed to know he'd have a new son. 'My lad will probably want to follow my footsteps into the SAS,' he assumed.

As we drove home from hospital after our ultrasound, Steve launched into more stories of out-smarting terrorists in Northern Ireland and Iraq while in the Special Forces, while I clutched our scan pictures to my chest and dreamed of the moment I would hold our little boy.

I vomited every day throughout my pregnancy but I didn't care. Didn't complain. It all seemed worth it to have a baby at the end.

When Stacey and Konrad were at school, Steve and I dossed around the house. I'd listen as he confided in me how serving in the SAS had scarred his mind. He falteringly told of the time he had to stick his finger into a bullet hole in his friend's guts to save him from bleeding to death. And he tearfully recalled seeing his mates blown to bits in operations that had gone wrong.

To cheer himself up he'd muck around with the two machetes he kept over the top of the front-door frame. They had been given to him by a foreign diplomat because he'd done such a good job of protecting him. Steve was clearly proud of them.

'Look how sharp these are, Dee,' he said. 'Look, I'll cut the palm of my hand, you cut your palm and then let's hold them together. Then we're blood brothers.'

I did whatever he said. I felt sorry that this big man who had been through so much had also lost his wife. And glad to have such a strong, worldly bloke protecting me: I was in awe. Because he'd had so many hard knocks in life, I understood why he was so protective of me. Flattered, even. He wouldn't let me out of his sight. Even when I was in the shower, he stood and watched.

'Now that I've found someone so precious, I don't ever want to let you go,' he'd say.

I'd never felt attractive until I was with Steve. He gave me so many compliments that I started to believe him. As part of his style and fashion advice, he persuaded me to ditch my thick glasses and, for the first time, I realised I turned heads whenever I walked into the pub with him (even if I couldn't clearly see any faces). That gave me confidence and made me happy.

Steve thought I was so gorgeous, so sexy that he worried other men would try to make moves on me. He didn't like any of his mates down the club talking to me and if I spoke back he snapped at me. 'Dee, you're here with *me*, not him.' I quickly learned that it was easier not to even look at other men because it would keep Steve's mood on an even keel. I'd sit there for hours with my head down, often falling asleep because I was so exhausted with the pregnancy and looking after Steve's house and kids.

Steve didn't like any of the few friends I had. He pointed out that he was so much more mature and successful so had nothing in common with them. Within months, whenever I went out it was only ever with Steve.

I hadn't noticed my social circles getting smaller. It was all part of my new life, starting afresh. My own family didn't have any time for me so I put all my attention and energy into Steve and his family.

Sometimes he and I would disappear for days, taking his caravan to Wythall in Bromsgrove, leaving Konrad and Stacey to be babysat by the lodger John, who lived in the cabin at the back of the house for the first six months I was there. Until one night, when he and Steve had an almighty fallout, which ended when Steve shoved John out of the gate and threw all his clothes over the fence. I never knew what that row was about but believed Steve when he said it was all John's fault.

Meanwhile, I felt I really was being looked after. Even though Steve could get a bit arsey when he was drunk, which was often, I could cope.

So I loved his idea of eloping to Gretna Green. He didn't ask to marry me in the traditional, down-on-one-knee way. Out of the blue while lying in bed, he said, 'Seeing as no one wants to know us, maybe we should just go to Gretna Green to get married and have a honeymoon at the same time?'

I didn't need an engagement ring, he said. The one he gave me on our first date would do.

He arranged everything. And on 7 July 1993, a week before my 17th birthday, I became Mrs Wilson. I wore a white and blue floral culottes suit with white shoes, all chosen by Steve. We married over the famous anvil and I felt fantastic, as if Steve and I were the only two people in the world.

The only other person on my mind that day was my real dad because I wished he'd given me away. And the only other person in Steve's head was Trish because, even though he'd bought me a £20 wedding ring from Argos, he said he didn't need a new wedding band because he already had one from her.

I knew from Konrad and Stacey's faces, and the fact that they were really quiet, that they were missing their mum too. But that day I felt we were more of a family than ever – all four of us had the same surname. Coming from a family of six, who had three different second names, that was really important to me.

No one mentioned my age or the fact my parents weren't there, except our witnesses. They were a couple we hadn't met before who were also lining up to get married. The bride-to-be, who was also called Denise, said, 'Ooh, you're so young and so pregnant. I bet your parents don't approve and that's why you're here?'

It didn't occur to me to call Mum and Dave to let them know I'd wed. I was an adult now, an expectant mum, and perfectly capable of making my own life decisions.

Our wedding breakfast was lasagne and chips in a pub. And our honeymoon was a few days in the caravan at Gretna with Konrad and Stacey.

I did not want or expect anything more. I was so happy to be married and so excited about becoming a mummy. No one could make me go back to living as a slave under Dave Angel's roof now.

Then everything changed.

A month after our wedding, Steve and I took off on a camping holiday in Devon. We loved driving for miles in Steve's Daihatsu, which was perfect for camping holidays. It had tons of space in the back for all our gear and, because it was a 4 x 4, Steve would drive it along the edge of the tide really fast and we'd laugh to see the car make high waves of water spray.

On the first night at the campsite, Steve had a skinful of rum at the clubhouse. I was sober because I was seven months gone.

We arrived back at the tent at 2am and I was shattered. But Steve didn't want me to go to bed: he wanted me to join him on a trek down a perilously steep, narrow cliff-side path to a beach called Otter Cove in the pitch black.

'Steve, no! You're drunk and I'm knackered. If I fall down that hill, I could really hurt the baby. I'm not going.'

His cajoling quickly turned to threatening.

'For fuck's sake, Dee, just a little walk! It'll be romantic. Trish would do it, Trish would have walked down there with me any time.'

But I would not go – my unborn baby boy came first.

It happened so fast it's hard to describe. Steve throwing down his lager can. Twisting his face with fury. Lunging at my belly and punching it.

I curled up into the foetal position in the corner of the tent while his fists and feet pounded into my back and head. I didn't care if he broke my spine as long as my bones could protect my baby.

His words, spat in red-hot anger, hurt just as much. 'You are nothing like Trish, you'll never be as good! You'll never take her place. She was a better woman than you'll ever be.

'Fuck you!'

I lay there, in a ball, until he ran out of energy to hit me anymore. Minutes later I heard his car start up and roar off.

I was terrified, mortified and in agony. I was in the middle of nowhere, where I knew no one and didn't even know the way back to the clubhouse in the dark. I rocked, holding my stomach. And I cried until I fell asleep.

I was vaguely aware of Steve's torch shining through the tent a couple of hours later but stayed perfectly still so he would leave me alone.

The next morning I could not look at him. And he could not stop apologising to me.

'I can't believe what I've done to you. I'm so sorry, Dee, but you do drive me crackers sometimes.'

'But what had I actually done, Steve?' I sobbed. 'All I said was I was tired because I'm carrying our baby. What have I done wrong other than saying no to a long walk in the dark while pregnant?'

'Dee, I said I'm sorry. It's all the SAS stuff – it gets in my head and makes me angry. Sometimes I fly off the handle. Sorry.'

Steve said he was too ashamed to take me to the hospital because the doctors would see that my back and stomach was black and blue. He said we didn't need to get the baby checked out because if I could still feel him moving he was OK.

We drove the four hours home in silence.

Holding both hands on my baby bump and feeling the flutter of my little one's movements was the only comfort I had on that journey. Because I had a horrible phrase turning around in my head: out of the frying pan and into the fire.

It wasn't so much Steve's slaps and punches that still hurt, wasn't so much his kicks to my ribs and head. It was his words during the attack, said through gritted teeth and with hot venom that chilled my blood – 'I hope the baby fucking dies!'

Chapter 5
No One Could Take Them Away From Me

Thankfully my baby did not die. Bret Michael Wilson was born at 2.40am on 26 October 1993, a 5lb 14oz tiny bundle with peachy skin and downy dark hair. The moment I saw him I was utterly overwhelmed with love.

I cried tears of pure joy when he came into this world. Seeing him, holding him, kissing him made everything horrible that had gone on before vanish from my mind.

Two weeks before my due date, after an evening at the club watching Steve play snooker and sink pint after pint, my waters broke in the chip shop.

A warm gush soaked my jeans and made a small pool on the floor.

I panicked. 'Bloody hell – what's happening to me?'

'The baby's coming – that's what!' said Steve.

I gripped the worktop in the shop as the pain came in waves. And after Steve had been served his box of chips and tinned roe he headed outside to tell a police officer I was in labour.

It was clear from Steve's staggering, slurred words and smell that he was drunk but the officer said, 'Follow me in the car and I'll put the blue lights on.'

I hung on to the handle above the car door all the way to Sandwell General Hospital while the contractions came faster and faster. By the time we reached the front door of the maternity wing the police drove off, but I was bent double and clutching at a litter bin full of fag ends.

Steve pressed the buzzer. And pressed it again. Then he bashed it before hitting it repeatedly with his clenched fist, getting more agitated within the few minutes we were waiting. He started rattling and kicking the door.

'Come on – for fuck's sake!' he bellowed. 'If you don't come soon she's going to have her baby in the dustbin.'

'Steve, they'll be here in a minute. Calm down.'

But Steve couldn't take it anymore. He swapped his fish supper to his left hand, drew his right arm back and punched the window next to the buzzer.

The ear-splitting sound of shattering glass made two nurses come running. As soon as they saw me they helped me into a wheelchair and tried their best to ignore Steve. He was swaying on the spot and, with chips hanging out of his mouth, shouting, 'If it hurts having this baby, it's YOUR FAULT!'

The nurses tried to make him lower his voice and quell his temper but no one could tell Steve, a former SAS officer, what to do. He stood at the side of the delivery room, noisily eating his takeaway while swearing and berating the doctors as they tended to me.

'No one leaves me and *my* wife waiting. I pay your fucking wages, I do. Paid my national insurance for years, which goes straight into your pockets, so do your jobs properly. Hurry up and get my baby out.'

When he was eventually called out of the room to speak to police about the smashed window, I was as relieved as the doctor and midwives. But when he returned I was mortified: because, while I was in the final throes of labour with my legs up in stirrups, he had brought Konrad and Stacey into the delivery room. He'd sent a friend to give them a lift to the hospital but they wanted to be there as much as I wanted them there.

'Dad, we really don't want to be seeing all this,' said Konrad.

'Whaaat? You don't wanna see your baby brother being born?' said Steve incredulously, as Konrad and Stacey turned away and left.

All the drama, tension and agony faded into insignificance as soon as the doctor held up my baby son and placed him on my chest.

I was euphoric. It felt so natural to hold my baby boy for the first time – like the two of us were always meant to be. Hearing him cry amazed me: he was so pure, so innocent, he instantly brought love into my life. Had I really made something so beautiful, so perfect? I thought a smile would never leave my face. I cared about nothing other than him: I was a mum, I had a gorgeous little boy and little else mattered.

Finally I understood the point of life. I had a reason to want to live forever.

Steve let me choose our baby's name so I called him after the lead singer of my favourite rock group Poison, Bret Michaels.

'Hello, my darling,' I said softly to him, nuzzling the top of his velvety little head. 'Mummy's going to look after you now.'

I had a son who really needed me. I was responsible for his entire being and would do everything I could to give him a happy life. He was already my greatest achievement.

Steve was immediately protective of me and baby Bret. And, although I was the youngest on the ward, I felt ready to be a mum.

It was a happy time for us, even though we had few people to share that with. None of the hospital staff wanted to swap small talk with us, thanks to Steve's window-smashing incident and the delivery-room verbals.

I could sense the disapproval from the midwives, so I was relieved to be discharged. At home I loved spending hours cuddling Bret in his soft blue blanket. Just staring at him in my arms or in his Moses basket made me feel more content than ever. Seeing Bret after his bath with his hair all fluffed up and wearing a bright-white Babygro with little blue ducks was the nicest sight of my life. I was tired, but happy tired.

Steve was a great dad. Any time I wasn't sure how to care for my newborn, he was right on hand with advice.

'You don't need to bother with all that breastfeeding palaver,' he said. 'Trish never did and look at her kids – perfectly healthy.'

Konrad and Stacey adored Bret and loved cuddling him but whenever my baby was in someone else's arms I wanted him back in mine.

My entire world had changed. But there was no great announcement about Bret's birth. I hadn't met Steve's parents or any of his extended family because he didn't get on with them – 'They're all horrible people, Dee. They hadn't bothered with Konrad and Stacey so won't be bothered with another child in the family. We don't need them in our lives.'

He didn't go into detail and I didn't press him because I was happy with just us. I loved life in our little baby bubble. I filled the days singing to Bret and making him promises.

'You're going to have everything I didn't have, my son – a comfortable home, a daddy. I'll even buy you a BMW when you're 21 because that's your name, Bret Michael Wilson.

'No one will ever harm you, darling. I'll make sure of it.'

Steve said he loved seeing me as a mum. He liked that having a baby made me more grown up. It made me even sexier, he said.

We had sex again only three weeks after Bret was born.

'Steve – give me some more time. I've only just had the baby.'

'Come on, Dee. You must've stopped bleeding by now; I remember that with Trish. I ain't going to have to find it elsewhere, am I?

'Stacey, look after the baby for a bit, will you? Me and Dee are going upstairs.'

It was painful. I was exhausted. But Steve said he needed me just as much as our baby did.

I was pregnant again almost straight away. Once again I was sick in the morning and, once again, Steve sat on the edge of the bath when I did a pregnancy test. I was thrilled to bits to see it was positive.

There were times when looking after a newborn while pregnant was tough. It could be uncomfortable carrying a baby on my hip when my bump was in the way. And it took Herculean effort to get up in the night to look after Bret when I ached for a good night's sleep.

I didn't complain, though. Life had taught me that pain was always inflicted as a punishment, whether it was deserved or not. But Bret had proved that, when it comes to pregnancy and childbirth, there can be something utterly wonderful at the end of a period of pain.

Brad Lee Wilson came into the world on 25 August 1994 and I was just as besotted. At 6lb 1oz he was bigger at birth than Bret but looked like his mini double. I loved my sons equally and overwhelmingly. Sometimes I wondered if you could love too much, if love could make you burst.

My two beautiful boys were born 10 months minus one day apart. But they were as close as twins.

Whenever Brad Lee slept in the travel cot in the living room, Bret's podgy little arms reached out for him. As soon as he knew how, Bret crawled over to Brad Lee's carrycot and peered down at his sleeping brother. If ever either boy wouldn't settle, laying them next to each other in the same cot immediately calmed them. And as they grew the bond strengthened: my two toddlers wanted nothing more than to be with each other.

I could not get enough of my boys. They were hardly ever grumpy and were smiley little things; probably because they had all of my attention all day. I got such a buzz out of dressing them nicely, playing peek-a-boo when they were in their bouncy chairs and seeing them splash wildly in their bath. Every time their dimpled little hands reached up to me or they treated me to a wide, gummy smile I melted. Double cuddling Bret and Brad Lee was my favourite way to spend time together. Rarely did I have one without the other on my lap. It was magical.

Steve was at home with me all the time. He loved his boys – I knew that. And I was glad to have him around. Although I took care of all Bret and Brad Lee's needs, I felt reassured that he was there in the background whenever I needed him.

'I'm much more experienced than you with kids,' he said. 'I'll just be here, watching you. And when you do something wrong, I'll let you know.'

It was expensive having two babies so close to each other. Bret hadn't had time to grow out of baby stuff to hand them down to Brad Lee. We needed two of most things. That's when I became aware that perhaps Steve wasn't as well off as he'd always made out. Not that I had ever seen a household bill. I was never told how much we owed on the mortgage, never saw a bank statement, never owned a cheque book or had any cash. Steve had the child benefit paid directly to him because I didn't have a bank account. He told me I needn't ever worry about money because that was a man's job. But, because everything for the babies had to be second hand, I had an inkling our purse strings were tightening.

In fact, Steve found one of the pushchairs discarded on the street so I had to scrub it down before Brad Lee sat in it. When I look at photos of the boys back then, I can see the towel sticking out from under him because the buggy was still wet. I notice tiny details like that because I look at pictures of my boys all the time.

I didn't see many friends; I didn't really have any. Even the odd one who still said hello if I saw them in town seemed babyish and boring now that I was 18 and a married mum-of-two.

I was encouraged by the health visitor to get out and meet other mums so I took the boys to toddler groups and enjoyed it when fellow mothers complimented me on my cute, giggly sons. Some said having two babies so soon would be their worst nightmare but it was a dream for me – I loved it. I didn't love sitting around drinking tea and eating biscuits with the other mums, who only ever spoke about how tired they were. Of course I was shattered too, but I'd been used to hard graft all my life so just got on with things.

I didn't consider looking after Bret and Brad Lee hard work anyway – it was something I loved and enjoyed. So I didn't make many friends at toddler group because, while they sat and chin-wagged or whinged, I preferred sitting on the floor and playing with my boys and the trains, trucks, trikes and tiny slides.

Back then, there was nothing else in the world I wanted or needed – just Bret and Brad Lee.

I was a good mum. I'd found my life's vocation, a focus for the future. Life would be good. Because I had my boys and no one could take them away from me.

Chapter 6
Jagged Pattern Of Life

Soon after Brad Lee was born, Steve upped his drinking. And when he was drunk, he was violent.

With two tiny babies I had little time for him. I didn't want to hear his SAS tales, couldn't be bothered pretending to be interested watching him play pool down the pub for hours. I just wanted to be with my boys, looking after their every need, being there for them always. In fact, I preferred reading *The Very Hungry Caterpillar* with Bret and Brad Lee on my lap, who laughed hysterically when I wiggled their titchy fingers through the tiny holes on the pages, than doing anything with my husband.

That made Steve fractious, needy and aggressive. I could usually tell when I was in for a slap because he'd start a row over nothing. And when his sentences included the word Trish, I knew a serious hiding was coming. But sometimes a punch would land on my face from nowhere, catching me before I could steel myself. He liked those attacks best – they were the ones that made all 5ft 4in of me hit the deck and made it easier for my 6ft husband to kick me in the chest, stomach, face.

Our lives fell into a jagged pattern. He'd beat me at least once a week then be full of remorse once he sobered up the next day. I didn't have any friends to notice my bruises, black eyes, swollen lips, limp. But people knew. Neighbours who heard my screams as my husband slammed me against the wall could never look me in the eye. Stacey and Konrad saw many of my attacks but interfering or objecting earned them a slap.

A friend of Steve's tried to intervene once but I paid double the pain price for that. Late one night he brought a group of his mates from the club back to the house to play pool in the cabin. And as he often did, Steve turned on me for no reason.

'You see this bottle, Dee?' he said, his lips twisted into a snarl. 'I'm going to smash it on this table then chuck it into your stupid face unless you fuck off.'

One of his friends jumped in front of Steve as he lunged towards me. He said, 'If you wanna do that to Dee, you'll have to do it to me first.'

His mates refused to leave until Steve had calmed down. And once they'd gone they called the police because they were concerned for me. With officers on our doorstep, Steve insisted everything between us was fine. He pulled me into what he thought was an affectionate hug, but was actually a headlock, to prove that all was just tickety-boo.

But Steve kept drinking after the police left. And it took only minutes before he blamed me for the coppers coming and inflicted what he believed was due punishment.

Back in the pool room he started fast bowling snooker balls at me. I leapt out of the way of the balls as they shot towards my head. But then he cornered me. After jabbing me with the cue, he then whacked me with it so hard that it cracked. He pelted balls at me with such force that he tired himself out and had to sit down in the corner, where he fell into a drunken, slobbering sleep.

I was a bloody mess. I could barely walk to the house and knew I couldn't manage the stairs so slept on the chair downstairs. When I woke the next morning my knees were as big as my thighs. It hurt too much to walk so I had to shuffle my way to the loo on my backside.

When Steve woke at lunchtime he looked stunned to see me with a badly swollen face and purple, double-sized legs.

'Oh my God, I've not done that?'

'You did, Steve.'

'No, Dee! I didn't mean it, you know I didn't mean it. Alcohol gets into my head and turns me into someone I don't know or like.'

That day he poured all of his rum down the sink. For the next three days I had to move around the house on my bum. A week later he was drinking and laying into me again. Such was the vicious circle of our life.

I didn't wallow in my unhappiness, I was strong enough to take it. After all, I'd grown up with it. I'd got used to the beatings from my stepdad so soon got used to them from my husband too. Besides, I had other things in my life apart from a husband who grew devil horns and fists of steel when he drank. Every day my aim was to make sure Bret and Brad Lee had a healthy and happy routine. I was thrilled to see my boys' first steps, both taken at only 10 months old. I felt overwhelming pride when I heard their first words, 'Mumma', 'Dadda' and 'Babba'. Even small milestones, such as growing out of a pair of shoes or tiny trousers, gave me a sense of achievement because I'd lovingly fed them every healthy meal that helped them grow.

Even when I couldn't see through both eyes because they were swollen from Steve's right hook, my clear focus was on teaching them, ensuring they knew they were loved and giving them the secure home life and set routines that help children thrive.

'Wassa matta with your eye, Mummy?' asked Bret, reaching out to touch my shiner.

'Ooh, Mummy just had a little trip on the stairs, love. It's not sore so don't worry.'

A gentle little kiss and squeezy hug from Bret, always the more sensitive of my boys, made all my aches fade away.

And the way Brad Lee could distract me from any woes with his cheeky humour made me laugh every day. 'Blue! And gween too!' he'd say, pointing at the bruises around my eye with a huge smile then clapping his hands as he'd been a good boy for knowing his colours.

My two babies were little boys now, with dark wavy hair, big brown eyes and eyelashes so long they lay on their chubby cheeks when they slept. Just being with them, stroking their dimpled little hands and landing 20 kisses on their faces made everything in my life OK again. Better than OK.

Seeing their faces light up and arms reach out when they saw me first thing in the morning showed me the only genuine love I had. When they fell asleep on me, their heads resting on my chest and arms stretching only halfway round my back, if I'd been frozen in time in that position I'd have been happy. Because in that moment the feeling of mutual trust and unconditional love healed everything that had ever wounded me.

The love I had for Bret and Brad Lee, and them for me, transcended everything and everyone else. I thought God had been tough on me in every other aspect of my life so he made it up to me by gifting me ultra-special little sons – magical little boys, Mummy's little angels. So I just concentrated on loving and looking after Bret and Brad Lee and focused on the hope they gave me.

My boys were so full of love that they made everyone around them melt. But Steve didn't think boys and their dads should kiss or cuddle. So, each time they held up their chubby arms to hug him, he'd turn away and say, 'Go to Mummy for a cuddle.' It meant I got twice the affection from them.

Unbelievable as it sounds now, when Steve wasn't drinking he wasn't horrible. In fact, he could be nice. Charming. Gentle, even. Life could be fun. There were holidays in Spain and a Mediterranean cruise with the boys, aged only two and three. Stacey and Konrad came too, but Steve always ensured they had their own rooms separate to ours and they tended to do their own thing during the day. Steve made it clear he wanted to spend time with his new family. I see, only now, that they must have felt pushed out. But I was too engrossed with Bret and Brad Lee to realise it then.

We travelled to beaches all across the UK with our boat tied to the roof of our car. Bret and Brad Lee loved being at the seaside. They'd work together as an industrious little team to make a city of sandcastles. It was always Brad Lee, the more extrovert of my boys, who would run to the sea to fill his tiny bucket so he could pour it into the moat surrounding the sandy city. Time and time again he'd toddle off to the water's edge, never tiring of the fact his river would immediately sink into the sand. And it was always Bret, the gentle little soul, who would shriek at the sight of a tiny crab. He was always the one to cry when his ice-cream cone fell on to the sand or his monkey of a little brother jumped on the sandcastles. And he was always the first to cuddle in to me as the sun lost its heat and he lost his energy.

Steve spent most of the time on holiday drinking while I played with the boys but it was very generous of him to take us all away. He could show affection too, in his own way. He'd make me surprise meals with candles. He would run me a bath with lots of bubbles, tenderly combing my long wet hair afterwards. 'Whenever I've hurt you, I've never meant to,' he'd say soothingly. There'd be a nice bottle of wine over dinner. And another – and then we'd yet again become sucked into the cycle of abuse. Steve's drinking always resulting in my beating.

We were nowhere near as active as we used to be in the bedroom. I tried to avoid Steve's touch, partly because I was so tired looking after two lively young kids and partly because I was now besotted with them and not him. That made him angry and frustrated… and prone to thumping me.

Sometimes he'd drink so much he wouldn't hit me for two or three days afterwards as he was so ill.

Space and privacy were at a premium in our two-bedroom house so Steve told Stacey to sleep in the caravan parked on the alleyway at the side of the house and Konrad to make the cabin his home. But we frequently went out or had holidays as a family of six. To anyone on the outside, at least those living beyond earshot of our house, we were a happy family.

That's why Gemma was so excited to be part of it at first. She was Konrad's girlfriend who lived just down the street with her grandparents. I liked her immediately because she was a lovely, bright young girl and had a lot of affection for Bret and Brad Lee.

Steve treated her to his best charm offensive when she first came to the house. 'Come around here with all your friends and we'll have parties. And if you and Konrad stay together as a couple let's all go on a big family holiday in the summer. Here, Gemma, have another beer.'

Gemma thought Steve was a gregarious, friendly dad and that our house was a fun place to be. She was 15 when she started dating Konrad and, in her eyes, seeing him with his own pad – albeit a shed at the bottom of the garden – was the epitome of cool. At that age the story about Steve pushing Konrad's teacher into the school swimming pool after a disagreement over his son's gym kit was hilarious. She loved that Steve held big barbecues each weekend in the garden when music blared and booze flowed. The neighbours never complained. They'd done so in the past. Many times. But Steve gave them so much abuse they never dared moan again. No one had anything to say to him because no one wanted any trouble.

We all quickly took to Gemma, and she and Konrad were clearly mad about each other. But it was only months before she learned, the very hard way, that after Steve's barbecue and beers came beatings.

The first time she saw the other side of Steve was the night she and I went with Konrad and Steve to a pool bar in Walsall called Fast Eddie's. Stacey stayed at home babysitting the boys and soon we both wished we'd opted to do that instead because that night Steve picked a fight with a bloke in the bar over nothing. Konrad never wanted to start fights but knew he'd be in for a good hiding from Steve later on if he didn't back up his dad. So within minutes it escalated into a mass brawl, with glasses smashed, heads slammed into pool tables and the sickening sight of blood on clothes, carpet and walls. Our evening ended in Manor Hospital's A&E department, where Steve and Konrad's wounds were stitched.

Once Gemma had seen Steve in monster mode, it was as if she was truly accepted into the clan. It didn't take long for her to realise that this was the Wilson family way. When we all went out together for a meal we didn't sit around the table chatting like the Waltons. We sat on the edge of our seats knowing that at any given moment Steve would kick off if he didn't like the food, service, the waiter's attitude or even the wallpaper. Once he trashed an Indian restaurant in Birmingham city centre so thoroughly, even smashing the front window, he got arrested. It was the norm for a Wilson night out to end up with at least one of us in the police station or hospital.

Steve had also developed an addiction to painkillers. When he was in party mode he popped four paracetamol an hour. Every hour. He insisted he needed to anaesthetise the pain of losing Trish. His body was so numb and drink-addled that he lost the sensation in his bladder and often wet himself. Or worse. And guess who had to soak and scrub his sodden or soiled jeans the next morning? My disgust at having to do that job makes me think I should have been more insistent that he stopped necking pills so recklessly. Sometimes I wonder if I didn't put my foot down hard enough because I secretly hoped he might one day overdose.

None of this was enough to stop Gemma moving into the cabin with Konrad. And it didn't prevent her marrying him at 16. That was Steve's fault – the pressure he put on Gemma and Konrad to get wed was constant and immense.

'Why don't you two just get married? Go to Gretna Green – it's lovely there. That's what me and Dee did, and look how happy we are. We could all have a two-week camping holiday in Scotland afterwards. I'll arrange it all for you.' He went on and on and on about it.

Me, Steve, Bret and Brad Lee were all there when Konrad and Gemma married over the anvil on 14 June 1997. Afterwards the teen newlyweds asked Steve if they could leave us all at the campsite to go out for a drink, just the two of them. Steve said, 'Course it is! Go out and enjoy your romantic first drinks as Mr and Mrs.'

But while they were out his mood soured. Because when they came back he really let them have it.

'We came all the way up here to see you two get married and spend time with you, and you think it's OK to go off and do your own thing afterwards? You think it's OK to leave us here while you two go off and enjoy yourselves? You think that's a nice way to treat your family, do you?'

Steve liked to wear people down until they were so weak it was easier for him to beat them up. And he beat Konrad up really viciously that night. Gemma screamed and begged Steve to stop. Her gorgeous wedding dress ended up heavily splattered in her new husband's blood.

Gemma's dad didn't speak to her for 18 months after the wedding. He was a successful businessman and always told her he didn't trust or like Steve. Gemma's mum had a serious drink problem and hadn't taken much interest in her life for a few years. But no one could have saved Gemma by then. She was too far gone – she was too brainwashed. By that stage she was even dressing like a Wilson.

Steve liked Gemma and me to wear the same clothes but in different colours when we went out – usually sailor dresses bought from a market stall that were eye-poppingly short. We had one in black and one in pink and had to swap them around. He insisted we wore our hair long, wavy, with huge flicks at the front and puffed out at the sides, just like Trish's. And when he bought some knock-off Tommy Hilfiger blue and white puffa jackets he ordered Stacey, Konrad, Gemma and me to wear one whenever he wore his. He thought we looked like a proper family mob that should not be messed with. Actually we looked like a ridiculous pit-stop team.

Gemma moved into the cabin with Konrad and they paid Steve £60 a week rent. She got a job alongside Stacey in a factory that made traffic bollards. Konrad worked in a factory making parts for lorries, but I doubt they saw much of their wages after forking out for Steve's astronomical rent. Steve was forever promising to extend the cabin and install all the fancy Sky channels, but he never did; they didn't even have a bathroom. He insisted Gemma, Konrad and Stacey asked permission to come to the house to use the loo and he even installed a three-way internal phone system so if I heard the phone ring twice it meant the cabin was calling; three rings and that was Stacey ringing from the caravan. It was embarrassing for us all.

'Dee, is it OK if I go to the loo, please?' Konrad would ask.

'Of course,' I always said. I wanted to add that there really was no need to keep asking, but that wasn't true. We all had to obey Steve's rules – or else.

Gemma, like me, didn't take long to work out that it was better to stay quiet when Steve was having a go at someone verbally or physically, otherwise you would be in his firing line. The poor girl used to have to watch in silence as her father-in-law pummelled her husband into a state of near-unconsciousness. But more often it was me she saw hitting the floor from one of Steve's right hooks. We all had to turn a blind eye, keep schtum and become very selfish for the sake of our own survival. All of us understood that, parts of us were glad it wasn't happening to us but none of us blamed the other.

Even Gemma felt the force of Steve's wrath. 'You two are so weak compared to Trish,' he'd say to us both at the end of a rum-filled night. 'You have a very low pain threshold. You'd never have made it into the SAS. Here – let's see how tough you are.'

Steve smashed pint glasses and beer bottles on to the kitchen floor and ordered us to walk over them in our bare feet. Gemma and I locked eyes for a split second. In that look, we both understood that we'd just have to do it or we'd get thrashed by him instead.

I went first – I gritted my teeth and tried to walk over the shattered glass as quickly and lightly as I could. As shards pierced into my soles my body hunched and buckled but I refused to cry.

'Pathetic,' said Steve, spitting with disgust. 'Let's see what you're made of, Gemma.'

Gemma took a deep breath and winced her way over the glass. She was so frightened she shook. After a few agonising steps she collapsed into a chair and cried as she pulled out large glass spikes that sliced into her feet – cutting her fingers as she did so.

Steve threw his head back and laughed. 'Konrad, your wife's not a patch on your mum, is she?' he said. 'Nowhere near as strong as Trish. This one's not good enough for you, son.'

One of his other favourite punishments was making me and Gemma hold our arms straight out in front of us while holding two five-litre water containers, which we used to take camping. If our arms dropped, he'd dig us in the stomach.

But that was nothing compared to Steve's worst attack on Gemma, when he threw a giant stereo straight into her face. He broke part of her eye socket.

'I didn't do anything – why did he do it?' she asked as I wrapped frozen peas in a face cloth to make a cold compress for her swollen eye.

'There's no reason, love,' I said. 'It was just your turn.'

Awful as it sounds, Gemma actually got off lightly. Steve was a bit intimidated by her dad so he couldn't batter her as hard as he battered me because she'd have told him.

'If my dad knew what Steve did to me he'd take me away from here immediately,' she said.

'Why don't you go – make a new life?' I suggested.

'Because I love Konrad,' said Gemma. 'And Konrad's too scared of his dad to come with me.'

I never knew if Gemma stayed with Konrad at Linden Avenue because she loved him and was trapped under Steve's evil spell. Or if, deep down, she thought she would stay long enough to try and get Konrad out of there.

Hearing her speak about her dad saving her from Steve meant, just as I'd done as a child, I let my mind wander to thoughts of my real dad who would one day rescue me and his two adorable grandsons.

Chapter 7
'You're Too Evil'

Steve was cruel most of the time but not all the time. Not every single day. In one of his kinder moments he helped me try to find my real dad. He said he would ask everyone he knew if they'd heard of Dennis Paige. One day he rushed back from the club and said someone had told him Dennis lived with a traveller called Geraldine on a site at Batman's Hill Road in Tipton.

'Come on, Dee. Let's drive there. You've waited long enough to see your real dad.'

I was thrilled. My heart beat at triple speed during the half-hour drive to Tipton. As soon as we arrived, neighbours outside helpfully pointed out Geraldine's pale-green static caravan. I could barely contain my nervous excitement and squeezed Steve's hand tight.

When Geraldine opened the door and clapped eyes on me she took a step backwards and paused for a second, then said, 'Well, I know whose daughter *you* are.'

I was elated. And a moment later devastated.

'Oh, babe, you're too late. Your dad died of angina 18 months ago,' she told me.

I was too stunned to cry. Too crushed. In all the hundreds of different scenarios that featured in daydreams of my real dad, he was always alive and waiting for me. It hadn't crossed my mind, even fleetingly, that he could have passed away.

Geraldine insisted we stayed for a cup of tea in her immaculate home. She was in her late forties, had dark-blonde hair, heavy jewellery and a warm, empathetic nature. She sensed I was distraught and did most of the talking as I was too choked.

She gave me a photo of my real dad and did her best to bring him alive for me with her stories.

'Your dad was a lovely fella,' smiled Geraldine, 'until he had a drink, that was. Then he'd become fierce, bad-tempered and trash this place. He'd wake up the next day and say, "Have we been burgled?"'

It was all too much. Hearing this about my father felt as if I'd been let down by the one person who could have saved me. Mum had said roughly the same things about Dennis, but I always tried to judge people on how I found them and not on hearsay.

Reluctant as I was to believe Geraldine, I couldn't doubt the word of a kindly lady who had spent two decades with my dad.

Geraldine told me the resemblance between Dennis and me was so strong there was no mistaking us for father and daughter. She'd seen me as a baby in a pram but never since.

As soon as her teapot and our china cups were empty I wanted to leave so I could have a good cry on my own. But Geraldine asked to give me one last gift.

'I read palms, love. You know, just to get by. Show me your hand and I'll tell you your fortune.'

I stretched out my arm over her Formica table and Geraldine took my hand in both of hers. Then her eyes narrowed and she dropped my hand as if it had scalded her.

'Jesus, I am so sorry Denise. I can't read your palm. I am sorry, really sorry. There is just too much... too much evil there.'

Geraldine jumped up from the table and said a hurried goodbye. And I felt rejected all over again.

Back in Steve's car my sobs came from deep within my stomach.

'Dee, she's a daft old bat. Don't believe a word she says – it's just gypsy hocus pocus,' he told me.

Learning that I'd never know if my dad would have been proud of me, that he could never warn Steve off hitting me, was an agonising blow. But whenever I was down, whenever I was knocked back, I would think, 'I still have my kids.' Bret and Brad Lee were always my focus – my world.

My life-long yearning for my dad made me vow never to come between my boys and their father. I knew that pain and would never inflict it on them. Steve was my boys' dad, even if he was an extremely strict father. He enforced SAS punishments on Bret and Brad Lee by making them stand with their arms outstretched and a Yellow Pages phone directory balanced on them for 20 minutes at a time. Or he'd make them lie on their backs with their feet raised two inches from the floor for 10 minutes.

'This'll toughen you up, lads,' said Steve. 'This is what it was like in the SAS. You're Daddy's little soldiers. One day you'll be as big as me and can be in the elite forces, just like me.'

His punishments were extreme but Steve never hit my boys. I knew he loved them and he knew I wouldn't want to separate them from him.

Although I hated the way Steve disciplined Bret and Brad Lee, I couldn't argue that it worked. Whether we were at the park, shops or out for tea, someone usually complimented us on our boys' impeccable manners.

Bret and Brad Lee would never interrupt adults. They would sit quietly through a meal and say please, thank you and excuse me in all the right places without being prompted. If ever Steve thought their childhood chatter was getting above polite conversational level, he'd click his fingers and they'd immediately fall silent, straighten their backs and fold their arms. Steve said his years in the SAS meant he would only tolerate behaviour befitting young officers in the elite forces.

No wonder they were rarely naughty.

To compensate for Steve's hard rules I was extra-soft. I spent my time with my boys playing, reading, singing and laughing – but mainly cuddling. I was glad both boys were affectionate or I'd have spent my days chasing them for hugs.

Bret and Brad Lee were my lights in an otherwise dark life. Being with them made me feel so content there was nothing else in the world I wanted. Except perhaps another child and all the extra love and light a little one could bring.

I'd have been thrilled to know I was pregnant in the summer of 1998. But I didn't know until it was too late. My periods had always been irregular, possibly because I hadn't had many before I got pregnant by Steve, so I was never sure if I'd missed one, two or even three. On our way to a bowling alley in Stourport, Steve stopped his car at a petrol station so I could get out and buy cigarettes for him and sweets for the boys. I'd been suffering severe stomach cramps all the way but mentioned nothing as Steve had little patience and zero sympathy for illness. But when I stepped out of the car I saw that my white jeans were covered in blood.

We drove straight home and I went to the toilet. I was in excruciating pain that left me breathless but that was nothing compared to the agony of seeing a tiny foetus lying there in the loo: tiny feet, tiny hands. Lifeless.

'Steve,' I sobbed, 'come here!'

'For fuck's sake!' he said, before coming into the bathroom and seeing me rocking with distress and wearing a blood-soaked towel wrapped around me like a skirt.

'I think I've had a miscarriage,' I sobbed. 'I think our little baby is in the loo.'

'Trish had a miscarriage too,' said Steve, peering down the pan. 'It happened by the side of the road while we were taking the motorbike on holiday. But she just nipped home for a shower, changed her clothes and went straight back out with me on the motorbike.

'She was younger than you are now so you've just gotta be grown up about it. Whatcha crying for? It's 'appened for a reason. It looks like a little girl. I think God doesn't want you to carry girls because you're too evil.'

Nothing he said could have made me feel worse than I already did. The sobs coming from me had a low, guttural sound.

'Chrissakes, Dee, keep it down!' he barked. 'We don't want the boys knowing you're making a fuss.'

He was right – I didn't want Bret and Brad Lee alerted to what had happened or to hear Mummy so upset. So I struggled upstairs, lay down on the bed, pressed my face into a pillow and howled.

Steve took the boys out for the rest of the day. I heard them leave after he'd flushed the loo.

For the next 10 days I bled but Steve would never let me buy sanitary towels. He said, 'Trish never had them – so you're not having them.' I made do by folding layers of tissue paper and laying them inside my knickers.

That summer, more than ever and without realising it, Bret and Brad Lee were my crutches who propped me up when I was down. I thought often and longingly of the little girl I wanted but couldn't have. And I imagined her with my pale white skin, brown eyes and jet-black hair and looking like a mini Snow

White. Whenever I watched *Snow White* with the boys on our duvet movie nights I always shed a few tears and would get a little hug from Bret, who assumed I was moved to tears by her jealous stepmother.

My boys' first day at school was the proudest day of my life. I welled up seeing them in their smartly pressed sky-blue polo shirts, grey trousers with a pristine seam down the front and Clarks' shoes, which were brand new but I'd polished anyway. Steve usually insisted the boys wore second-hand clothes, but even he knew they needed spanking new clothes for school. He was forever banging on about living in a posh area and he didn't want the boys standing out for the wrong reasons at school. Walking them to Grove Vale Junior School that day, I felt a good six inches taller.

'Even though I'm a big schoolboy now, I'll still miss you, Mummy. But don't worry, I'll play with you when I get home,' said Bret, giving me his tightest hug as their first school bell rang. How typical of my elder son to console me at a time when his nerves must have been all over the place.

'I'm gonna show the teacher my Spiderman bag,' said Brad Lee, who showed only excitement and not a flicker of anxiety on such a big day for a small boy.

All parents must feel the same on their children's first day at school. But when my two took each other's hand, looked back and blew kisses at me, even the other parents said, 'Aww, so cute.'

The school had never had siblings in the same class who weren't twins. And after their first day they came home wearing a sticky label bearing each other's name. 'The teacher said she couldn't tell us apart so we thought we'd trick her and swap our names,' giggled Brad Lee. He was such a little imp.

I feigned shock and Bret's eyes widened. 'We'll tell her the truth tomorrow,' he said. 'It was only an accident, Mummy.'

I laughed so hard my stomach hurt.

That first day at school, when we asked another parent to take a picture of me and Steve with our dapper little sons, also gave me a sense of accomplishment that we were still a family unit. Despite everything we had gone through, we had stuck with it and come this far. My boys had both parents waving them off.

In the pictures they brought home from school there was a mummy and daddy there. I was usually drawn in a flowery pink triangular dress with an arch of black hair and a giant red smile. The boys depicted themselves as the same height with giant circular hands that looked like balls of wool. And always they drew Steve as a much smaller, greyer figure with a straight or sad mouth. But at least the pictures painted a traditional family set-up, something solid and sought-after. I loved sticking those pictures to our fridge door.

Tolerating Steve's rampages seemed a price I had to pay for the precious times with Bret and Brad Lee. To be with them, to give them the happy and fulfilled family life I wanted for them, I had to put up with Steve. Like Mum said, I'd made my bed and had to lie in it.

Chapter 8
Leave, Return, Repeat

Sometimes I just could not cope.

Asda in Great Barr is just over the road from Old Oscott working men's club, which was Steve's favourite drinking den. It was highly unusual for me to be allowed in the supermarket on my own, but Steve said he'd leave me and the boys to get everything on his shopping list while he had a few pints in the club.

A couple of hours passed and he still hadn't turned up to pay at the till. I knew Steve would be bullying people at the club into drinking with him by buying them booze. That was how he made so-called friends, who were in reality just fellow drinkers reluctant to stand up to the man who could start a fight in an empty room. Steve would be telling them about cutting carotid arteries, throwing grenades, killing with Kalashnikovs. He would be well oiled by now. And that meant one thing: a kicking.

I don't know if it was the sickening inevitability of what I would get back home that did it, or seeing the happy couples push their trolleys around the supermarket. Or the sight of the other mums shopping, who were trusted with money and free to make decisions about simple domestic details that I could never do. But in the middle of the aisles I was gripped by fear and an urge to flee. Not just the store, but my life. I wanted to run away – *had* to run away. Immediately.

I abandoned the trolley, grabbed Bret and Brad Lee's hands and ran to the phone box. A sticker above the shelf advertised a free phone number for Women's Aid.

'I have to get out of here,' I said, breathing heavily as panic rose through my body and made it shake. 'I need to get as far away from here as possible.'

The woman on the phone was amazing, like a guardian angel. She arranged for a taxi to pick us up at Asda and take us to a train station where we could collect pre-paid tickets.

'We're going on an adventure, kids,' I told Bret and Brad Lee as we boarded the train for Llandudno, Wales.

We sat around a table on the busy train and were soon joined by a friendly, smiley lady. The boys immediately warmed to her and it seemed she was charmed by them, too. They drew her pictures and wrote her notes in rainbow-coloured writing with the crayons and drawing pads I always carried in my handbag. The lady did a wonderful job of convincing Bret and Brad Lee they were the best pictures she had ever seen in her whole life.

'Where are you off to, boys?' she asked.

'On an adventure with Mummy!' they said, grinning with excitement at being on a train and going somewhere new.

The lady seemed so lovely, so gentle, I found myself whispering the real story to her. That we were running away from my violent husband and, although we had no money, I was feeling more optimistic about life than I had done in years.

'I wish you all the luck in the world,' she said. 'Your boys are so beautiful, so happy and polite, that I can tell you are a wonderful mum. And you are so young. I hope you have lots of happiness ahead – you deserve it.'

I remember the lady on the train really well. The kindness of strangers meant a lot to me. Especially then, when I needed to be bolstered. She gave me extra strength that day.

A taxi met us at Llandudno station and we were driven through the countryside to a women's refuge. It was dark by the time we got there. We had a lovely comfy double bed and two singles, but we all huddled together in the big bed. At dawn I woke to find Bret and Brad Lee sitting on the deep window ledges, looking out at sheep in a field.

'It's nice here, Mummy,' said Bret, wide-eyed. 'Can we go out to play with the sheep?'

I felt safe there. The staff told me I need never go back to Steve and said they would help me find somewhere to live in peace.

A life without having to endure my husband's attacks seemed like a dream. My boys and I would have few material things but we'd be free of violence and aggression – and that was far more valuable to me than any fancy car or foreign holiday. They loved being in the same class at their local school and shared many little friends, so I vowed to find them a school and friends that were even more fun. I would do everything I could for my boys.

The women in the hostel tried their utmost to persuade me not to return to Steve. 'Men like that promise the earth but rarely change,' they said. 'We advise you not to go back – but it is your decision.'

I knew I needed to heed their warnings. But I could not inflict the pain of not having a daddy upon Bret and Brad Lee. Hard as I tried and as horrible as he was, I could not put them through that. Being fatherless caused me unending agony that I couldn't let them suffer. It seemed beyond cruel.

So I let Bret and Brad Lee call Steve from the hostel phone. That's when the blackmailing began.

My boys silently nodded as Steve told them he loved them, missed them and wanted them and me home. 'Tell Mummy, if she doesn't bring you back, there won't be any nice holidays no more. Mummy won't be able to look after you properly on her own. We can't be a family if we're apart.'

After the call, Bret and Brad Lee said, 'Mummy, why won't you go back to Daddy so we can all be a family?'

'Daddy is sad without us. Will we ever see him again?'

It worked. Four days later we were back at Linden Avenue.

There were hugs for the boys on the doorstep and promises to me about quitting drink. And then, two bottles of wine over dinner and two black eyes before bedtime.

That was the hellish rhythm of my life. There were a few ups and lots of downs, then more downs. I left Steve eight times. Each time I put up with hours of being slagged off while he necked rum, beer or wine through the night until he dropped, usually in the early hours. I was always so relieved to see him drop. I'd take a couple of quid from his pocket and hide it among the boys' toy shelves until I had around £12, which was enough for a taxi fare to the nearest women's refuge. Then I'd gather the boys together in their warm pyjamas with their favourite teddies, step over Steve while he snored in a drunken heap on the floor, and strap my sons safely into a taxi outside. Each time I was adamant I would never go back. But Steve knew I'd eventually relent and let Bret and Brad Lee speak to their daddy. He knew he'd get to me through them; that we'd be back.

Once, in a women's hostel in Oldbury, I opened the curtains on our fifth morning there to see Steve in his Daihatsu outside. He saw me, started up the engine and beckoned. I will never know how he traced us.

'I have good contacts in the SAS,' he said as we drove home. 'I'll always be able to find you, always hunt you down – especially if you try to take my kids away. I'll never give up.'

Between the bad times I loved being at home with my boys. But bullies always aim to destroy what you love so, to ruin those happy times, Steve said I had to go out to work to earn enough money to keep the house. I knew nothing about our household income but he said we were short of money because I'd stopped him going on SAS missions.

That was true. I urged him not to go on tour with the Special Forces. I was too worried he'd be killed by terrorists and would leave my boys with the same empty ache I had for a father.

Steve said it was my fault we were skint so I had to make up the loss of income. He drove me around the streets so I could go into shops asking for work.

I got a job in a chip shop and worked noon to 2pm, then 5pm until midnight for five days a week. I'd never known Steve to have a job but while I was sweating out my shifts at the chippie he stayed home all day with the boys and I missed my little ones terribly.

But my sons and I had such a close relationship that sending me out to work meant Bret and Brad Lee enjoyed our time together even more.

'When Mummy comes home it's the funnest times *ever*!' they'd tell Steve.

Whenever my boys said something affectionate about me, which was often, Steve never said anything. He just kind of snorted.

If I'd had a good friend, perhaps they'd have given me perspective. Had I stayed close to my mum and sisters, maybe they'd have forced me to see sense. But there was no one around to offload to, no one who could possibly understand me or listen while I got everything off my chest about my husband. There was no point in making new friends because Steve always ruined my friendships by belittling, insulting or threatening anyone he felt got too close to me. So even though I'd never had him in my life, I missed my real dad.

After yet another 2am attack, which stopped only when Steve passed out and slumped to the floor because he was so pissed, I ran out of the house and into the pouring rain. I had no money for a taxi so walked eight miles to the Tipton Cemetery, where Dennis is buried. I just needed to be near him, I didn't care that it was pelting down.

When I got there the gates were closed so I sat outside, shivering and drenched. As daylight broke, an elderly man from a nearby house came out and asked what was wrong. I told him all about Steve – it's funny how you can talk to strangers. He tried assuring me that there were refuges for women like me and they'd help me leave Steve, but I told him I'd tried all that. He asked me to come inside and get warm and I thanked him yet declined because I wanted to be as close as I could to Dad. So he gave me a blanket and cup of tea and I was touched at a rare sign of humanity in my world. Just like the lady on the train, that man reminded me that kindness does exist.

After a few hours I asked him to please call Steve to pick me up and take me home.

'Where have you been? Who are you with?'

Soon I wished I'd stayed out because Steve could be as vicious with his words as his hands.

'Leaving me like that. Trish would never have done anything so stupid. You thick little cow!'

Steve measured everyone against Trish, even her own kids. Konrad and Stacey had no time to grieve for their mum in their own way.

'If you had a bit more of your mum in you, maybe you'd have turned out better,' he'd jeer at Konrad.

'Look at these pictures of your mum, Stacey. Didn't she have a gorgeous body? She really looked after her body, she was so sexy.' As if a young girl wanted to hear about her mother in that way.

Steve rubbed their faces in their dead mum – literally.

At the end of most nights when he'd been drinking, he got out a blue box which held Trish's jewellery, pictures and ashes. He'd open the wooden casket and run his fingers through the ashes, saying, 'Oh, my darling Trish, I'm here for you.'

He'd haul me, Stacey or Konrad over to him, smear her ashes across our mouths and force us to eat them. 'Here you are, try this. Eat it! There are pieces of Trisha in here and it might do you some good.

'Come *on*, eat your mum's ashes. Show her you love her. Let's get Trish's ashes inside ya, a bit of her might rub off on to you.'

He'd pick out all the black lumps from the ashes and tell us those were her cancer. We ate them to save ourselves a beating, then we'd feel petrified we too had cancer.

He really was evil.

Considering Konrad, Stacey, Gemma and I all endured hell with Steve, it might seem inevitable that we'd unite against him. But Steve was an expert at creating divisions. He'd stir up rows then stand back and enjoy watching the spectacular fallouts that ensued. To divide and conquer, he'd tell Stacey I'd been running down her mum – something I would never have done. He'd tell Konrad I'd been slagging him off and wanted him to leave our home. That was another lie. He even insisted I beat up Gemma over a petty row about a car and when I refused he gave me a hiding. So the next time he ordered me to attack Gemma I agreed.

'Pretend I'm hurting you,' I said under my breath to Gemma as I started grappling with her in the cabin.

As she screamed and cried out in fake pain, Steve shouted from the garden, 'That's right, Dee – give her what she deserves! Really lay into her.'

We all knew Steve was at the root of every conflict between us but didn't stick up for each other as much as we should have: it was every man for himself.

Steve's violent rampages always happened in the small hours of the night when the beer ran out. We would all have to stay up drinking with him until he dismissed us with insults of being weak and a lightweight. Attacking one of us was his way of ending the night and going to bed feeling like a winner because he'd left one of us in a bloody heap. He had to be in control.

Konrad, Gemma, Stacey and I always unlocked the back door of the cabin so whoever was his target at the end of the night could run. Konrad would sneak out and leave his Citroën Saxo car at the top of the road with the door open and the key under the seat so we could make an escape. Even though he was working and had money, Konrad was still too scared to leave his dad's house for good. We all were. Fear kept each one of us there.

Whenever Steve lashed out, he lay low for a few days afterwards. We knew we were back in his good books when he cooked for us. A plate of chips with curry sauce or a baked potato with beans and cheese would be laid out for us on the kitchen table.

Whenever Steve was out, Gemma and I fantasised about how to do away with him. We hoped the canal at the bottom of the steep-sloping bank would finish him off.

'Maybe, the next time he drinks himself into a coma, we could just roll him down the bank and he'd plop into the canal like a piece of sewage,' we said.

You know how people love to talk about what they'd do if they won the lottery to cheer themselves up or give themselves a surge of hope? Imagining getting rid of Steve was our equivalent of the lottery conversation.

Chapter 9
Fleeing The Barbed Wire Nest

Steve promised us family holidays as if dangling a carrot in front of our faces so we'd tolerate being beaten by his stick. But all carrots eventually go off and our last holiday was truly rotten.

We both enjoyed the *Godfather* films. He liked the gory bits and the merciless violence, whereas I empathised with the gangsters' wives, who were always living in fear and being caught in their men's crossfire. So Steve announced that we would all go to Sicily. He loved to make out that he generously paid for all his family to go. But that was never the case. Stacey didn't go to Sicily because she couldn't afford to pay her own way.

'It'll be great – all that red wine and pasta,' he said, patting his wobbly stomach that was already bloated with beer. 'There'll be lots of ice cream for you, Bret and Brad. Konrad, me and you will try the Italian beer while Gemma and Dee look after the kids. We'll have a ball.'

Few families would opt to travel to Sicily by bus, but Steve did because the SAS man was scared of flying. And he never minded long, arduous journeys if it meant he could drink every mile of the way.

After a few hours of beer swilling on the bus he was blotto. He went to the loo on the coach so many times that it stank and a few passengers moved closer to the driver and away from the putrid smell at the back. Then things turned nasty.

The driver, annoyed at having to repeatedly stop the bus to empty the loo and exasperated at having the other passengers' endless complaints about Steve in his ear, had a word. He said to Steve, 'If you didn't drink so much and I didn't keep having to stop, we would all get there a lot quicker.'

Bad move.

Steve, now fuelled to the point of violence with booze, was incandescent with rage. 'Who do you think you are? You're not driving fast enough, that's why this journey's taking so long. I can take this bus off you – I'm SAS. Shift out the way, I'll drive us.'

Steve slapped the driver and tried to barge his way into his seat. The female tour guide intervened and calmed Steve down by insisting she'd call the police and he'd be jailed if he tried to drive the bus drunk. Steve stewed in a huff for the rest of the way there.

But he couldn't stay out of trouble when we got to Sicily. He insisted that as a member of the SAS he also had top-secret Mafia links. In restaurants he tried to enthral us with stories of garrotting rivals and shooting them at point-blank range in their beds, but actually he just sickened us as we tried to eat our spaghetti pomodoro in peace. So he attempted to engage the local waiters in Mafia chat instead.

'Ciao! Are you, howa you say, Mafiosa? You think-a theez eez Mafia country? Noh! I was in the BRITISH Mafia.'

It was mortifying. And dangerous, especially when he tried pushing around local restaurateurs who looked like they shouldn't be messed with. In the end there was only one restaurant we could go back to, and even that was embarrassing. One night, poor Bret had a terrible fright when a striped ginger stray cat jumped out from the bushes and towards our table. I don't know if Bret thought it was a tiger – but he had diarrhoea through his shorts and we were sitting on wicker chairs. The next night we had to go back there for dinner because Steve had been thrown out of the other restaurants and they gave us plastic chairs.

During the daytime Gemma and I spent hours on the beach with the boys while Konrad was ordered to drink with his dad. Gemma was so good with the children, which is why I know just how devastated she was when she had a miscarriage not long after we got back. After a couple of days in hospital she came home to Linden Avenue, white-faced with red-rimmed eyes and clearly heartbroken.

I could not believe what Steve said to her. It was word-for-word exactly what he had said to me when I was in the same sad situation – 'Trish had a miscarriage, too, you know. We were on a motorbike holiday and she had the miscarriage at the side of the road, had a quick shower later on and got straight back on her bike. She was a lot tougher than you are, Gemma. Konrad, you've got yourself a weak one here, lad. What a waste of space.'

Steve punished Gemma for her weakness by not talking to her for days and treating her like a leper. Being criticised for losing a baby added to her devastation, but at the same time Steve staying away from her was a blessed relief.

When Konrad told his dad he couldn't drink with him throughout the night because he needed to be with Gemma, Steve hit the roof. 'Henpecked, that's what you are! You're going to let a woman tell you what to do? You're going to let your wife walk all over you? Are you a man or a mouse?'

The relationship between Steve and Gemma was clearly worsening and Konrad was stuck in the middle, torn between love for Gemma and fear of his dad. It was highly stressful for us all.

Meanwhile Gemma was finding it harder to keep quiet about Steve's brutality. One day, when Steve was showing off with his machetes, he boasted that they were so sharp they could give Konrad a new hairstyle. But instead of cutting Konrad's hair he stuck the blade deep into his son's neck. It was a gruesome cut that left a gaping hole. I felt sick at the sight of the flesh hanging out of his neck and Gemma was horrified. She rushed Konrad to hospital for extensive stitching and was absolutely furious at the entire depraved situation.

Steve never apologised to Konrad or Gemma – not once. But taking a chunk out of his son's neck was one of the few attacks that made him feel guilty. And whenever he felt bad about anything, he took it out on me. That evening he started pulling me around by my hair, then used his machete to hack it all off.

Seeing my waist-length, thick black hair lying in heaps on the floor made me cry. I had never in my life had short hair, yet now it looked just like Jodie Foster's when she chopped it all off in *The Accused*. It was so short it felt spiky to touch and wasn't even long enough to cover my ears.

The next day I asked to go to the hairdressers to get it properly styled. But Steve refused to let me and insisted on tidying it up himself with kitchen scissors.

No wonder Gemma was desperate to leave Steve's house, but by then she was trapped because she was pregnant.

Loren was born in June 1998, perfectly healthy and gorgeously pretty. Gemma and Konrad were thrilled to bits. We have photographs of Steve holding Loren in hospital and looking like a proud granddad. I adored Loren, even though it felt weird to be called 'Nan', aged 23. But it was good to get pictures of us all together like that. Because not long afterwards Gemma left with Loren and never came back.

There was no warm homecoming for Gemma and Loren when they came back to Linden Avenue. Instead, Steve greeted them with a warning about paying their rent.

'Your rent still needs to be paid even if you're off work. You know that, don't you, Gemma?' he said ominously. 'I can't afford to subsidise a family of three in the cabin. If you can't pay up, you better ship out.'

Within a fortnight of Loren's arrival Gemma had to start working late shifts in a chippie not far from where I worked. She'd barely had time to get over the shock of giving birth and would drag herself off to work after being kept up all night by a sleepless baby or a drunken Steve, who held his beer and pool parties barely a metre from their bedroom out at the cabin. I wanted to cry for her. Unfortunately, I knew exactly how she felt. But like I said, we didn't stick up for each other because we were all too scared.

A few weeks later everything came to a head. Steve demanded that we all went to a blues club in Handsworth late one Saturday afternoon. You couldn't tell him you didn't want to go, you had to do as he said or face his violent consequences. So, while Konrad and I reluctantly yet obediently followed Steve into the club, Gemma stayed out in the car with baby Loren, Bret and Brad Lee. Steve said we'd only be an hour.

But that hour turned into four. All that time Gemma was in the car and had to feed nine-week-old Loren cold milk. While she was out there a group of thugs surrounded and rocked Steve's car and demanded she gave them money and jewellery or they'd turn it over. She was petrified and all the kids were screaming.

When Steve stumbled out of the club he didn't care that Gemma was shaking in a weeping, frightened state. 'For God's sake, you've got to man up a bit, Gemma. Stand up for yourself more. You're such a lightweight,' he told her.

How on earth he expected Gemma to single-handedly scare off a bunch of violent idiots while holding her tiny baby and looking after two other small children is beyond me. Steve insisted he would drive us all home that night, even though he must have been five or six times over the legal limit, hitting every kerb, churning over people's front lawns and swerving to miss trees and lampposts by an inch.

'Someone is going to be killed in this car,' said Gemma, clinging to the door handles and trying desperately to safely cradle Loren in her arms.

That night Gemma decided she'd had enough. She tried to wake Konrad but he was too out of it with drink. So at 2am she grabbed a few things for Loren and fled to her grandparents' house. A few hours later she caught the first bus to her dad's house and never came back. It was years until I learned how Gemma had fled. But the morning after we were all stunned by her disappearance.

'Where the hell is she?' demanded Steve when he and Konrad woke around lunchtime and realised Gemma and Loren had gone.

Gemma's grandparents were lovely but Steve made abusive phone calls to them at 1am, threatening all sorts unless they told him her whereabouts. He wasn't angry about her leaving, he was angry at his losing. Thankfully, no one in Gemma's loyal family ever gave any clues about where she'd gone.

Konrad was heartbroken, Steve was furious and I was envious. Gemma had escaped Steve's warped world with her child. I dearly wished me and the boys had gone with her.

Chapter 10
'Welcome To The Wilson Family Home'

Gemma's mum came to Linden Avenue the day after she fled. She arrived with the intention of patching things up between Gemma and Konrad, at least for baby Loren's sake. The very fact that she even attempted to smooth over something so dangerously rough made me suspect that either Gemma hadn't explained the true extent of her hell at the house, or her mum didn't believe her. Because if Gemma's mother had understood the harsh realities at Linden Avenue she'd never have set foot there and certainly wouldn't have tried to pave the way for her daughter and granddaughter's return.

Steve welcomed her in with open arms and gave her his full-blown charm offensive.

'Well, hello! Welcome to the Wilson family home. Why on earth haven't you been here before? We should have had you over for dinner and drinks way before now. You've hardly changed a bit since school, you know. You were a year above me, weren't you?'

Steve went on to speak warmly of their old mutual friends, none of whom still spoke to him.

'Come on back to the pool room, where all our parties take place. We have amazing times out here, you know. Real good laughs. You should come next time – we'd love to have you here. I mean, you're family. You're part of the clan, the inner circle.

'See this cabin? And the pool table? Aren't Gemma and Konrad lucky to have a lovely place like this to themselves? Especially since I'm just on their doorstep whenever they need my help. I wired up special phones so they can let me know whenever I can do anything for them. I built this cabin with my bare hands, you know. I'm a proper handyman. I was just about to refurbish the whole cabin and get Sky installed for them before Gemma took off.'

Steve had no intention of doing any such thing. Not without tripling Gemma and Konrad's already sky-high rent anyway.

'We miss Gemma, we really do. She and Konrad are such a lovely couple. Doting young parents, too. It's a real shame you weren't at their wedding. It was beautiful, you know. Really romantic.'

There was no mention of the wedding reception and the far-from-dreamy ending, which saw a blood-splattered bride and beaten groom.

'We've had lovely family holidays together, too. We like to travel together, all the family. You should come along next time.'

Steve omitted the small matter of his tendency to pick full-blown fights with most of the people he met abroad. He even beat up Konrad when he and Gemma dared to go clubbing in Sicily without inviting him.

'Here, have another glass of wine.'

Steve was well aware that Gemma's mum was an alcoholic. Which is precisely why he kept talking and refilling her glass with wine, rum and then beer. After a few hours, she was blotto.

She probably didn't even hear the door knock or notice Steve leaving her out at the cabin while he went to open the front door. On the doorstep Steve was faced with Gemma's nan, who had called round because she was worried her daughter had been gone for hours. She was in her seventies and suffered badly with arthritis but still had a fighting spirit. But when she started telling Steve exactly what she thought of a man who had bullied and beaten her granddaughter, Steve reacted as he always did when confronted: he became violent. He shoved Gemma's nan, a frail pensioner, with such ferocity that she fell flat on her back on to the stony driveway with a bone-crunching thud.

Now fizzing with fury, Steve's fake charm offensive vanished and it was the real Steve, evil Steve, who stormed back to Gemma's mum at the cabin. He immediately started running Gemma down to wind her mum up.

'Gemma was henpecking Konrad – always nagging, always moaning, always bossing him around. He's the victim here. Konrad has been under Gemma's thumb. He's done all the work with Loren but Gemma's lazy and weak. This mess is all her fault.'

Gemma's mum was a feisty lady, especially when fuelled by booze – which is exactly why everyone who knew her tried their utmost to keep her away from alcohol. There was no way she'd sit quietly and listen to Steve slagging off her daughter. So she gave him a piece of her mind.

But, despite Steve's insistence that she was a member of his family, she wasn't used to the Wilson family ways. She didn't yet know that he would never let anyone stand up to him, backchat or even disagree with him.

At first his attack on her was verbal. 'What the hell do YOU know? You are nothing but a useless old alcoholic – an ancient old alkie. Gemma won't get away with breaking up my family and taking our Loren. I will hunt her down, I'll make her pay. She'll be sorry she's done this to my son, I'll make sure of that.'

Gemma's mum didn't know what was coming. She wasn't aware, or sober enough to realise, that when Steve backed you into a corner he was about to launch the second stage of his attack. As she slumped against the wall Steve began poking and jabbing his finger into her as if adding full stops to separate each of his rapid-fire insults.

'You are a worthless old drunk. No wonder your daughter's so weak. She's a waste of space, she's a loser like you. You interfering old nosey cow. Stupid. Ugly. Bitch.'

Gemma's mum didn't know to keep quiet for her own sake. She hadn't learned that her safest option was not to resist Steve's assault. So when it came it was merciless. Like a crazed animal, Steve laid into Gemma's mum with a flurry of kicks and punches. Even when she collapsed to the floor the brutality continued. His fists rained down on her stomach and chest. He stamped on her head and booted her in the face.

The blows stopped only when Steve needed to catch his breath and slug more beer. But anyone who had seen him in full psycho mode knew that Gemma's mum was being treated only to a temporary reprieve. More beer would rev him up to the next level of aggression. The next one-way boxing bout was imminent.

Stacey knew that only too well. Although she lived in the caravan and was still working in the factory, she was adept at keeping out of Steve's way. But that night, risking her own safety, she saved Gemma's mum. She opened a door at the side of the cabin, bundled her out and helped her run all the way to the bridge on Linden Avenue. Luckily, Steve had slid to the floor in a drunken stupor by the time she got back. Because I dread to think what Steve would have done to Stacey had he known she'd helped an enemy – the idea is too terrible to contemplate.

Gemma's mum was covered in cuts and bruises from head to toe. She had two black eyes, a badly smashed-up nose and a seriously swollen lip. She called the police but I never heard the outcome of that complaint. Gemma's nan was very badly shaken up. If Konrad and Gemma's marriage hadn't been dead before then, it certainly was now. A few days later, Gemma served divorce papers on Konrad when he was at work.

'Don't sign them, son,' said Steve. 'Rip them up into a thousand pieces. Let's set fire to them. Why the hell would you give her what she wants? Make her wait, make her pay. And why the bloody hell did you marry her anyway? She's not good enough to be a Wilson – never was. She's no daughter-in-law of mine.'

Splitting up wasn't going to be easy for Gemma and Konrad with a baby involved. Gemma served more papers on Konrad asking for custody of Loren to be jointly shared between her and her father.

Steve loved getting the court papers. He revelled in the thought of any kind of fight, any promise of conflict. He insisted we all turn up at Dudley Magistrates' Court to support Konrad on the day in June 1999 when Loren's custody was to be decided. So Steve, Stacey, Konrad, Bret, Brad Lee and me were all ordered to dress in smart 'court clothes' and turn up mob-handed.

We saw Gemma outside the court with her dad and she looked broken. She was thin, pale and nervous. Steve loved picking on vulnerable people so honed in on Gemma's tense emotions by insisting we follow her into the court waiting room.

'Look at Gemma, boys. Doesn't she look weak? She's going to get an awful fright when the judge hears what Konrad has to say. Won't it be nice to have baby Loren back with us all the time?'

Steve's over-confident pre-hearing mood soon vanished when Konrad came out of the hearing. He had objected to handing over joint custody to Gemma and her dad and instead insisted on applying for full custody, just as Steve had told him to do.

But the hearing was adjourned to allow background reports into Gemma, her dad and Konrad to be compiled. Steve took fright then – he didn't want anyone digging into his business.

As we left court that day, Steve was gleefully looking forward to jeering at Gemma and her dad outside. But in the end security guards had to escort them out of court and to their car. It worked, because Steve didn't say another word to her.

We didn't get another day out in court when the second hearing was called. In fact, no one turned up at the next hearing – not even Konrad. So in the end joint custody of Loren was granted to Gemma and her father. Thank God. That was definitely the best decision all round. I was working hard enough to look after Bret and Brad Lee and I didn't think I'd have coped trying to protect newborn Loren from Steve's hellish home life. Loren was far safer away from Linden Avenue.

Eighteen months later, Gemma again served divorce papers on Konrad, this time at home. He wouldn't sign them either, out of spite: his dad's spite.

'Don't ever do what a woman tells you to do,' advised Steve. 'If she wants a divorce, you tell her to go and screw herself!'

Chapter 11
Reaching Out And Fighting Back

I took an awful lot from Steve. But I was not a simpering little limpet who let myself be thrown around. I was painfully aware that it was better not to fight back with words or blows because I'd always come off worse. But sometimes I could not help it.

When Steve went on and on about Trish, there were times when I shouted back, 'Well, I'm not Trish, am I?'

That cost me a punch in the mouth.

After years of hearing him gush on about the ghost of his wife, I once yelled, 'I wish you'd died instead of Trish.'

That won me a head butt and a broken nose.

Steve said the reason he battered me so much was because it annoyed him when I cried. So after that head butt I laughed.

'You think you're funny?' said Steve. Then he dropped his head into my face again. My nose was broken in two places.

I struck back physically, once. One afternoon in April 2000 I was sitting on the living-room floor, cutting the vinyl straps that bound a pile of *Great Barr Observer* newspapers, which I delivered to 150 houses each week for the grand sum of £8. Steve stormed home in a fury because earlier I'd dared to suggest he shouldn't spend all day getting drunk at the club since he needed to pack to go to Spain the next day.

'Don't you ever tell me what to do,' he said. 'I care more about my drink than a stupid fucking holiday!' Then he booted me so hard in the coccyx I thought my back would break. In a flash, I spun round and stabbed him in the arm with my scissors. They were big scissors, strong and sharp enough to cut through the tough plastic packaging straps around the papers, and they sliced through his forearm until they reached bone.

'Look what you've done, you evil cow,' said Steve, stunned to see blood dripping from his deep wound. 'I could send you to hell for this. I'm gonna tell the police what a madwoman you are.'

I didn't care, I wanted him to call the police. I was not sorry, and I would immediately confess to officers what I'd done and explain it was self-defence. I'd show them the bruise on my back that matched the toecap shape on Steve's boots. I would tell them about every black eye and broken rib I'd had.

But Steve did not phone the police. Instead, he went to the kitchen, got some strong black cotton, then sat on the edge of the bath and stitched his skin back together. 'The SAS trained me to do this better than any stupid doctor,' he boasted. 'I'm like Rambo, I am.'

Violence was such a common occurrence in our house that the fight was no big deal and next day we went to Spain, as planned. And it was a good holiday. Steve, as usual, spent most of his time there in the pub, which left me, Bret and Brad Lee to have lovely times together on the beach. I adored seeing them play football with the Spanish kids and felt so proud to see how easily they made friends despite the language barrier. They always looked so cute in their little shorts and sun hats. In those moments I could almost convince myself that life would be OK.

If you saw us as a family packing up Steve's car to go to Dorset each Christmas, where we stayed in log cabins, which Santa visited on a sleigh, you might have been tricked into thinking everything was idyllic. What no one saw was Steve insisting I could only spend £20 on gifts for each of the boys when they were four and five years old. I went into a pound shop, bought little cars, a bow and arrow set, colouring books and bouncy balls and felt awful that it was the best Steve would let me do for our sons. Yet on Christmas Day when Bret and Brad Lee saw their 20 tiny packages they were thrilled. They were always so grateful for anything, so appreciative. They were never spoiled or demanding.

The following year, Steve gave me more money for presents and I bought my boys colourful little green toy 'Palm Power' laptops, which helped them with sums and spelling. But Steve refused to give me any money to buy wrapping paper. On Christmas morning I told Bret and Brad Lee that because Santa had so many children around the world to visit he didn't have time to wrap their presents. I felt I'd failed them.

The next year, Steve again insisted there would be no wrapping paper. So I wrapped my little boys' presents in newspaper. Steve could spoil even the most idyllic family times; he always had to try to show he was boss, that he held all the power. He had to try to ruin the bond between my boys and me, which I knew was unbreakable. Sometimes I wondered if he was jealous that we had so much love for each other.

No matter how hard I tried to be positive and tell myself everything would work out in the end, the reality would jump up, bite (punch, kick or slap) me and shatter that fantasy of living happily ever after.

I felt a surge of hope when I heard, from a lovely lady at yet another women's refuge, that she thought she knew where Gemma lived. I felt sure Gemma would take me and the boys in because, if anyone knew just how much we had suffered at Steve's hands, she did. But when I got to the tower block of flats and asked the security man to buzz her door, Gemma wasn't in. So I returned the next day with a note, which the security man promised he'd deliver.

Dear Gemma

I really hope you and Loren are well. I missed you both when you left Linden Avenue. Konrad, Stacey and I got blamed. But I am so glad you ran away because at least you are safe now. Things got a lot worse after you left. I am desperate to find somewhere for me and the boys to stay where Steve will never find us. Do you think we could stay with you here, even just for a little while? Please? We're pretty desperate. Please leave a text just saying yes or no on my mobile and I'll know whether we can come or not.

Thanks, Gemma. Hope to see you soon.

Dee X

When I didn't get a text from Gemma the next day I wondered if she hadn't yet received my note. But when I hadn't heard from her two weeks later I had to accept that she couldn't let me and the boys stay with her. I didn't blame her. She was finally free of Steve and having me, Bret and Brad Lee there might have blown her cover and left her and Loren vulnerable to an attack.

Meanwhile, back at home the level of Steve's ferocity cranked up a gear. In February 2001, I had the worst attack of my life. I never actually knew what pettiness had sparked the bust-up – that memory must have been booted out of my head. But Steve's savage brutality is still horrifyingly acute; it still haunts me.

Bret and Brad Lee were playing in the pool room at the back of the house. And I am so grateful they did not see their daddy drag their mummy by her hair face-down along our drive. I'm glad they did not see him kicking me every step of the way. Or the trail of blood my scraped face left in the path up to our back door.

I desperately wish they had not seen me after the attack, so bloody, swollen and grotesque that they looked at me and asked Stacey, 'Who's that?'

Steve dumped me on to the hall floor and locked the door from the outside. Trembling, sobbing and coughing up blood, I scrambled to the phone and called 999 – 'Please come to 20 Linden Avenue, Great Barr. Quick!' That's all I could say before hastily hanging up. I couldn't explain more because I was in too much pain to talk; I was drifting out of consciousness and scared in case Steve caught me calling the coppers. He would have killed me.

Officers arrived minutes later. They knocked on the windows and doors and shouted, 'Are you OK in there?' I was too scared to shout back.

The back door rattled as Steve unlocked it. He ran to the hall, where he hauled me up from the floor, dragged me to the bathroom, dumped me in the bath and hid me behind the shower curtain. 'Stay there and shut the fuck up!' he spat, before leaving me to open the front door.

I heard officers ask if they could come in and look around. As their footsteps neared the bathroom, I heard Steve say, 'There's no one in there.' But an officer saw my reflection in the mirror, called an ambulance and arrested Steve.

This time, while in hospital with concussion and severe facial injuries, I pressed charges against my husband. While Steve was in prison on remand, Stacey visited me on the ward: Steve had got to her.

Stacey said, 'If you don't drop the charges, I'll end up in care and we'll lose the house. And because you can't afford the mortgage on your own, Bret and Brad Lee won't have a roof over their heads.'

So I dropped the charges. I told the police a group of lads wearing hoodies jumped me – that's what Steve told me to say.

When you're beaten up so many times, memories of each attack blend into one another. They blur, just as my eyesight did when my face was rammed against a stone wall, over and over again. But I can remember every blow of that battering, every kick to my stomach and stamp on my head. It scarred my mind more than many of the others.

Because while I was in hospital, Bret, the son Steve always called his weakest boy, said something at my bedside I shall never forget.

'Mum, if Daddy ever hurts you again, I will kill him. The first thing I'll do when I grow up is bash him to stop him hitting you. I won't let him hurt you again, Mummy.'

It made me cry. I knew it was said out of love for me but it still scared me.

Did Steve know that his middle son was only seven but was growing physically stronger and more determined to fight back?

Chapter 12

'If He Loved You, He Wouldn't Make You Do This'

Stacey did a bunk from Linden Avenue one night in March 2001. Steve had an argument with Trish's nephew, who'd come over to visit, and, as usual, he escalated the row until he was making wild threats of violence.

In the madness of it all, Stacey must have slipped away. Because she disappeared from the caravan and never came back. As far as I know she never spoke to Steve again. Not long afterwards Konrad went to work in the factory as usual but never came home. We heard he had moved in with some of Trish's family.

Steve had demanded that both his kids paid him for their board. Now they'd run off, he was short.

'It's your fault my kids left,' he said, prodding my chest. 'You'll have to make up the lost money. You'll have to get another job.'

He said I hadn't earned enough with my five nine-hour shifts each week at the chippie; that I didn't work hard enough and that's why I lost my chippie job.

But that wasn't the reason I didn't work there anymore. I had a good working relationship with the chip-shop owner, Michael, but that infuriated Steve. Michael and I were far from flirty and only ever platonic but Steve didn't believe that.

He waited for an excuse to have a go at him and one night took exception to the fact I had to wear a cap to work – even though I'd worn one on every hour of every shift for years.

Steve waited for the chippie to close, then pounced on Michael, beating him up and smashing every window of his BMW.

Michael didn't exactly sack me after that but he told me he couldn't keep my job open. I couldn't argue – I felt so sorry for him and was mortified about what Steve had done.

Steve said I had to get a new job pronto and that pretty much the only thing I was good at was giving massages.

'I've set up an interview for you in a massage place in the city centre so smarten yourself up and let's go.'

I dressed in a navy skirt suit and white blouse in an attempt to look as professional as I could. I wasn't qualified in massage and would have to talk my way into the job.

Once I arrived at the place I shall call Sensations, I was immediately impressed. It was a pretty upmarket place. The interview room had posh-looking swag curtains, thick blue carpets and trendy cream sofas. It smelled of cleaning products and Shake 'n' Vac.

My interviewer was a glamorous lady in her fifties with jet-black long hair, a deep tan, heavy make-up and lots of gold jewellery. She seemed warm, friendly and almost motherly. The interview didn't take long. She just looked me up and down and told me I could keep £100 of the £120 the clients paid for an hour with me. That was fantastic money – I was stunned.

Then she wanted to know my height, bust and dress size.

'I'm a dress size eight to ten,' I said. 'Is that for my uniform?'

'We don't wear uniforms here, love,' she said, writing my sizes down in a little black book. 'But clients like to know these things before they pick a girl. Come on, I'll introduce you to the others.'

My interviewer unlocked a clunky metal door that opened into a bar area. That's when it hit me.

One girl was dressed in a see-through negligee. Her friend was wearing a minuscule skirt and bustier. And over on a sofa flirting with a bloke was another girl in a tiny schoolgirl outfit.

I was in a brothel.

'Steve, bloody hell – that place is full of prostitutes!' I said as soon as I got back into his car. 'I can't work there. No way!'

'You can just do massages, Dee,' he said. 'You gotta or we'll be repossessed.'

I begged Steve to let me find another job. I swore I'd find one that paid just as well but didn't degrade me. Wouldn't it be better if I only slept with him? Wouldn't we all be happier if I got a nice job in an office?

Steve phoned Sensations that evening and told them I'd start the next day.

I sobbed the whole way there but, since I obviously wasn't like the other girls, I wouldn't do what they did.

'You think you can just do massages here, love?' said one of the girls, eyeing my suit and exchanging looks with the others. 'You've got no chance. You have to be ready to give clients extras if they ask for it. Here, have some condoms.'

I felt sick. And then I phoned Steve.

'Please don't make me do this. I can't do this.'

'You've got no choice, Dee. If we lose the house, where will the boys live then? Just earn lots of money tonight to keep the boys secure and we'll talk about it later.'

I don't have a clear memory of my first punter. Experiences with customers are fuzzy, just like recollections of all the beatings. But I know it was horrible, just horrible. More than anything I was scared: I hadn't been with another man since I was 16. I felt like I was cheating, even though I had a despicable husband. I was a mum, I had two lovely kids and yet I felt even more worthless than in all my history with Steve or Dave Angel. It was a new low. I knew there were ways to make money without having to sell every shred of dignity I had left but not in Steve's mind because the money was unbeatably good.

And so five days a week, from 11am until 8pm, I worked at Sensations. Steve bought me short dresses cut obscenely low at the bust. They were always buttoned down the front as I learned that yanking a dress over my head and yelping as my hair tangled around the buttons didn't really do it for customers.

Steve bought all my clothes and underwear. He got a sick kick out of buying me the tartiest, skimpiest clothes he could find.

I had two babies and thought my body was sacrosanct. But my husband saw it as something for sale. I was 25 and confident about my figure because Steve bought me weights and taught me the SAS way to do sit-ups; he said it was important I kept my body looking good for him. But actually he saw my body as an investment, a money-making tool. Even though my husband was whoring me out, I still felt I was betraying him as I bared my body to total strangers.

Back home after each torturous shift I scoured myself in the hottest shower I could bear before I would even let Bret and Brad Lee see me. I would not allow the depravity of that job to contaminate their innocence and purity.

Thoughts of settling my boys into bed each night, snuggling in between them to read a bedtime story, got me through each shift. Feeling the genuine warmth of my boys' cuddles after being treated like a piece of meat all day kept me sane. Hearing my beautiful sons say 'Mummy, I love you more than infinity' erased the hours of filthy sex talk that punters had salivated into my ears. Bret and Brad Lee idolised me and I adored them. They gave me the only true love I had in my life and I loved them back with every cell of my being.

Thankfully, they knew nothing about the disgusting reality of Mummy's new job. They believed I was a waitress and were glad I was home every night to tuck them in.

To keep home life separate from work life, all the girls had fake names when we were at Sensations. I picked Sadie because it has the word 'sad' in it – that's how I felt during every foul moment of that job.

Each shift began with me and the other girls sitting on the sofas until a customer showed some interest in us, then we'd be called into the bar area, where we pretended to socialise with them. When a punter said, 'Are you ready?' that meant we'd been picked and we led them off to a private room before asking for the money upfront.

There was a £10 room with a basic massage bed, or a £20 room with a Jacuzzi. Punters paid £50 for half an hour and £120 for an hour.

Clients were not down and outs who saved their dole money for a couple of weeks as I'd always assumed. They were barristers, police officers, managers – top-notch people who happened to like paying for sex. Having them on top of me, sweating on to me, was utterly disgusting. Vile. I hated every second. I had to close my eyes and go somewhere else in my mind because otherwise I'd have been sick. Using my imagination to take me away was the only way I could guard my soul.

Most customers wanted a massage until they were aroused, then they'd put on a condom and it would be wham bam, thank you, mam. Some liked to be tied up, whipped and smacked for the dominatrix experience. Others wanted pervy things like a schoolgirl and teacher role play.

The regulars I had didn't like rough stuff – they liked me being quite soft, almost matronly, with them. But there probably isn't a working girl in the world who, when in the extremely precarious position of being alone in a private space with a stranger who thinks he has bought ownership of you, hasn't endured violence. And I was no different.

The man who tried to anally rape me was a new client. There were no safety buzzers or cameras in the room, no bouncers to come running when I screamed. Instead, it was left to the other girls to burst into the room and chase my attacker away.

I had never been so scared. And we never saw him again.

Despite scrubbing myself clean in a hot shower between each customer I always felt stained and grimy. Even after the punters who didn't actually want sex.

Unbelievable as it sounds, a good few men turned up just for a chat and gentle touching with girls who were paid to listen. We called it 'the girlfriend experience'. Some of my regulars, who liked that sort of thing, seemed like pretty decent blokes. Whenever they asked why a nice girl like me did the job, I explained that my husband made me.

'If he loved you, he wouldn't make you do this,' one of my regulars said. 'You don't deserve to be treated like that.

'If you were mine, I'd never let you go. I'd treat you so well you'd forget all about that husband and this job. I could take you away from all this.'

Bullshit. That was exactly what Steve had said too. I trusted no one but learned to smile and look interested.

Steve loved picking me up outside Sensations in the car every night because as soon as I saw him I had to hand over every penny of my earnings, which after a few weeks were up to £700 a night. I was not allowed to keep a single penny.

Earning nothing from a quiet shift wasn't a smart move for me. I'd genuinely had no punters in on one Friday and was relieved because at first I thought earning no money could be my way out of this hell. But that evening when I got into Steve's car and reported zero takers he was apoplectic. 'No money, nothing at all – you've been out all day working and have nothing to show for it? I need cash for tonight's drink. You'll be doing something about that.'

Bret and Brad Lee were asleep in the back of the car. They were always tired out after a week of school. And I am so, *so* grateful for that. Because with my two sleeping sons in the back seats, Steve drove me at breakneck speed to Cheddar Road, which is Birmingham's red-light district.

'Earn your money out here then, you dirty whore,' he said, leaning over to open the passenger door and shoving me out of the car. 'Do not come back until you have some cash on you.'

'Please, Steve, do not do this to me. Please, I'm begging you. I'll earn twice as much at Sensations tomorrow, please! The boys are in the car – don't let them see me do this.'

But Steve locked the car doors and jabbed his finger towards the group of women by the road, bending themselves into s-shapes at the kerb-crawling cars.

I had learned that, when Steve was in a rage, the best way to survive was to grit my teeth and get it over with quickly. I never won our fights. Arguing fuelled his temper. Objecting riled him into beating me harder. And so with Steve's car in sight, and my beautiful boys in the back, I talked to men through their driver windows until one sharply nodded and gestured for me to get into the passenger seat. It was, at that point, the worst half-hour of my life.

Steve got his £80 drinking money. And I was sick out of his car window during the drive home.

From then on I worked hard at Sensations to make sure I was picked. Having sex over and over again was often painful but I could never show that, never rest. At least I wasn't afflicted with the agony of an STD because we always insisted on condoms and had free sexual health checks at clinics every month.

There was little relief after each shift because Steve asked me every disgusting detail about each punter. Even if I'd had a jump-on, jump-off job, he wouldn't believe me. I had to make up all sorts of titillating stories just to feed his twisted sexual fantasies.

He wanted to know everything about the other girls who worked there too. Some were junkies, selling their bodies for their next fix. A few had tough-guy pimps, who terrified them into the oldest profession in the world. A couple were teenagers and far too young to realise what they were doing. Others were Albanian girls controlled by gangsters, who were always turning up and starting a ruckus. The odd one worked to support their families, just like I did.

But I was the only one pimped out by her husband.

Generally, the other girls were a bitchy bunch. Catfights over money were common. One girl called Jade was a bully and we suspected she stole cash from us. Each time she was accused she would overly protest by saying, 'I swear on my son's life I didn't take your money.'

But I knew she was the thief among us so when some of my earnings were pinched I confronted her and got the usual 'I swear on my son's life I didn't touch it'.

I'd had enough. 'Listen, Jade, stop saying that about your son, because one day you will tempt fate.'

She curled her top lip, looked at me like I was a piece of crap and seemed ready for a fight. 'Who do you think you are?' she said. 'You're no better than me, you stupid slag!'

I kept my cool. 'Don't treat me like a little tart. I do this for my family. And I'm not going to stand by and let you steal my money and take food from my sons' mouths.'

The manageress heard our exchange and called me into the office a few hours later. She said she'd seen that I stood up for myself, kept a level head, was polite yet wouldn't stand for any messing around. Because of that, and the fact I always handed over her share of the takings (while others pilfered some of theirs), she offered me a job as a manager at another massage place I'll call Fingertips.

I suppose I was a madam, which doesn't sound nice. But it meant that, as long as I made sure there were enough pretty girls staffing the rooms every night, the money was stashed in the safe and the place was spotlessly clean and locked up at 4am each day, I made £1,000 a night. Cash. The best bit by far was that I didn't have to sleep the rooms anymore.

All my money went to Steve. I never had so much as a fiver in my pocket. But Steve got greedy. He didn't want to see the punters' money going to anyone else. So, even when I was manager, he made me sleep the rooms too.

'Now you're a manageress you have to look the part,' he said, buying me an £80 dress from a shop called Glitz in Walsall, which was a black knitted number with a *Playboy* bunny logo emblazoned across the chest. As if that made me more respectable.

Then Steve got even greedier. He thought he could run his own escort agency. He had cards printed on black paper advertising 'Hot Lips Escort Agency' with his mobile number written in bright pink and gave them to taxi drivers and his mates down the club.

He said I could see punters in the cabin in our back garden. Thankfully, I only had to spend time with one customer there. He was an Asian man who wanted a massage and full sex. He paid me upfront and as soon as I got his cash I obediently slid it under the door to Steve, who was lurking on the other side.

He was certainly not the worst client I'd had. But the fact I saw him at home, inches from where Bret and Brad Lee usually played, made me again vomit afterwards. I refused to see anyone else there.

Normally, Steve would never let me refuse him anything but around that time, because I was bringing him lots of money from Fingertips, he laid off with his beatings. I wouldn't attract customers with a stitched lip and punched-up eye, now, would I?

Steve treated himself really well with my money. He didn't splash out on a holiday for me and the boys, because that would have meant my having time off. Instead, he bought himself two more diamond rings and stocked up with lots of booze. He must have spent a fortune on antique guns just so he could show off with them, like he did with the machetes. He even bought himself some alloys for his beloved car.

Steve also paid for a family membership to David Lloyd's gym, which was the only spending that had any benefit for me, Bret and Brad Lee. The boys enjoyed going there to play badminton and loved the curly fries in the bistro. I worked out every day and was really fit. Whereas Steve went there to chat up women he said were 'fit for shagging'.

He even insisted we went there on the social nights held especially for singles and divorced members. I'd be there but wondering why as I was a married mum of two; I'd have to pretend I was enjoying myself while Steve chatted up loads of other women. And I'd squirm with embarrassment to see him pile on the fake charm, pull out his best lines and cheesy compliments before buying them drinks. If only they knew what he was really like.

But some people knew. Once, while I was having a coffee at the gym with make-up covering yet another black eye, a man came over to have a chat. It wasn't flirty, but maybe could have been if I hadn't been so terrified. I was always too scared to look other men in the eye because if they'd shown me any interest Steve would have pulverised them.

'Ooh, someone's had an accident – what's happened to your eye?' he asked. But before I could reply with my usual lies about being clumsy and always tripping over, he said, 'Did you run into your iron man's fist again?'

I daren't talk to him again after that.

Chapter 13

In A Few Days We'd Start A Happy New Life Together

'I've been thinking, if you're cheating on me with other men, I should be able to have sex with other women. I have to relieve myself sometimes. What's good for you is good for me. I don't see why you should get all the excitement.'

Excitement? I hated every moment of being with strange men. And Steve knew that. He knew I ran to the shower numerous times a day to rid myself of the punters' aftershave, sweat and worse. In a move that utterly repulsed me, he took my money and spent it back at the Fingertips massage parlour on women who were by then my friends.

He confessed to that six times. And he took great pleasure in telling me whom he'd picked and what they'd done. He had full sex with Nikkita, a slim and quiet mixed-race girl whom he said was 'OK-looking'. And he had what he called 'hot sessions' and 'amazing shags' with four Albanian girls.

The last time, he even said that his girl was 'nice and tight downstairs because she didn't have no kids'.

That was it, the final straw. I hated the job, hated what I'd become, hated him; the endless batterings, hospitalisations, verbal abuse. The broken arm, the strangulations, the pillows over my head until I passed out. The control he exerted by seizing the household income. The disgusting way he had started holding me down and making me give him sex on tap, then forcing me to sell it to all and sundry. I had put up with all of that. But in the end it was the mental torture that got too much. Using my earnings to buy sex from my staff finished me off. He slept with far more than six girls. In fact, he spent most of my money and his day buying sex because, other than the gym membership, my boys and I saw no improvement in our lifestyle despite the thousands I'd earned in the previous 10 months.

Steve was trampling all over the very core of my soul, wringing out every last drop of self-respect I'd desperately clung to throughout my years with him. There was precious little left for him to steal before I lost my mind.

In those rare times when he could be nice, I told myself he controlled me because he loved me. When he rammed his fingers so far up my nostrils that blood spurted out, I tried to understand that his traumatic time in the SAS had given him a terrible temper. In those gut-wrenching moments when a fat, hairy, saggy and sweaty man lay naked on the bed and expected me to pleasure him, I reminded myself I was only a prostitute to provide for my family.

But this? Staying with a man who pimped me out, then used my money to buy sex with women I worked with and boasted about it? No.

I'd had enough. I had to get away from him before the degradation killed me, before his utter lack of compassion made me sink into his hell. I could not let Bret and Brad Lee see that their father was a morally bankrupt lowlife.

By now my contempt for Steve was deep so I didn't even argue with him about his sex sessions with the other girls. I didn't beg him to stop drinking or beseech him to take us both out of the seedy world of prostitution. I was too far gone for that. I abhorred him too much. Nothing he could do would make me want to salvage our so-called relationship.

Instead, I secretly and intricately started plotting my final escape. This time I would make watertight plans. I'd work out every detail until it was impossible for Steve to hurt me again. Leaving in the dead of the night with no money and no plan had never worked before. This time would be different, final.

I couldn't work at Fingertips once Steve had indulged in my colleagues' custom. I tried, but I couldn't stand the pity in the eyes of the girls I was supposed to manage. Life had taught me to keep my head up and feign strength and pride even when I was broken inside but once he demeaned me to such a black depth I just wanted to curl up and die.

I was shocked when Steve agreed, without argument, that I could quit Fingertips. He immediately found me a new place to work in a poky little flat above a shop in Bilston. I told myself that now I wasn't just working to support my family – I was earning to ensure my boys and I could leave Steve.

I met a girl there, whom I'll call Tanya, and liked her immediately. She was a single girl working to live, not to feed a drug habit or pimp, and this was the only job she could get. Three years younger than me, at 22, she was bubbly, warm and one of the most genuine people I'd ever met.

Between punters we shared our life stories. And I told her all about Steve.

'Why do you put up with it?' Tanya asked. 'Don't let him belittle you like that.'

I trusted Tanya enough to share my plans to run away with Bret and Brad Lee. She kept £200 cash I'd earned so Steve couldn't get his greedy hands on it. He'd have smelled a rat if I'd taken any more money because I had to list all the punters I had each day. He then checked my tally against the cameras that filmed anyone entering and leaving through the front door so he knew for sure I'd given him every penny of my earnings.

Tanya kindly offered to let me and the boys stay with her until I sorted out a place for us to live.

I knew my sons would never choose their dad over me. They had never seen him beat me, because that usually happened in the early hours when his home supply of booze had topped up what he'd necked at the club. But they had seen the bloody and bruised aftermath of his pent-up SAS aggression, although I rarely admitted I was a victim.

'Mummy slipped on the wet floor in the kitchen.'

'Mummy fell down the stairs.'

'Mummy wasn't paying attention and walked into the cupboard-door handle.'

My boys had heard every excuse I could think of, but they knew I was the gentle one and Daddy had a temper. I was the one who told them I loved them because they were wonderful, smart, clever boys. He was the one who disciplined them so they could be SAS men.

After years of denial, excuses and being blinded by fear, my focus was now clear enough to look at my life from the outside. I would see a solicitor about a divorce and insist Steve only saw Bret and Brad Lee under supervision.

By then I detested him so intensely I felt my brain was constantly frying with fury. I shuddered with disgust when I heard he had been getting Viagra pills on prescription and selling them at the club for £20 a time.

'Listen to this, lads,' he boasted so loudly that no one could ignore him. 'I told the stupid doctor I had erectile dysfunction syndrome and she believed me. Silly cow! But I need these pills to stay rock hard all day. I've got a lot of girls to see, a lot of things to do. Now, who wants one?'

He was even trying to sell sexy underwear at the club, probably because he bought lingerie for me from the market in bulk. Or he bought it knock-off. He was a perv and our entire life was now sleazy. Looking at him, listening to him and having him touch me made my skin crawl. I loathed him.

Saturday, 2 February 2002 was the day I decided to leave for the last time. All morning and afternoon I pretended everything was OK. And as evening came I made the boys' tea, gave them a bath and read them a bedtime story after they'd stayed up slightly later than usual watching TV. I tried to be chirpy and not look crooked at Steve because if I annoyed him the evening would not pass without a fight.

I feigned a headache and went to bed early, but could hear Steve clambering about the house, swearing to himself and the telly as he drank into the early hours. When the noise stopped I knew he'd passed out.

I hastily packed some jeans, tops and undies into a rucksack and pinched six £20 notes from the pocket of Steve's jeans, which was my money anyway. By 3am I was ready to leave for the last time.

As I'd done each time before, I would gently wake the boys, ease their jackets on over their pyjamas and bundle them out into a waiting taxi – each of us tiptoeing out the door and down the gravel drive. But when I opened the door to Bret and Brad Lee's room I stopped dead: Steve was asleep on the floor between their single beds.

I wanted to take my boys. Desperately. That was my plan. Looking at them lying there, Bret cuddling his pillow and Brad Lee sleeping diagonally across his bed, made me ache with love. But if I woke Steve and he saw what I was doing, he'd have gone ape and probably killed me. It struck me in that moment that, if me and the boys left together, Steve would get to me through them, but this had to be the time I left him once and for all.

So I made a snap decision to leave without Bret and Brad Lee. I didn't even kiss my boys goodbye because I was too scared of waking their father on the floor. That's why I sobbed in the taxi all the way to Tanya's flat in Bilston. Even though I was leaving my evil bastard of a husband and even though driving away was the start of a fresh new life, I was distraught.

Tanya stayed up to let me in. 'Why are you crying? You've done it – you've finally left him,' she said.

'I know, Tanya – it's just that I hated leaving the boys.'

After a strong cuppa and soothing words from her, I started to feel safer and more settled.

'Dee, you've done a brave thing,' she told me. 'You've left now and it's time to put all the plans in place. You'll have your boys with you in no time.'

'I'm never going back there,' I vowed. 'Not for anything. I just need my boys and we'll start a new life together.'

It was 10.30 the next morning when Steve rang my mobile, and that unsettled and wrong-footed me. He was calm. The volley of expletives I'd expected didn't come. He didn't threaten to batter me; he didn't swear he'd kill me.

'So there's no chance of you coming home?' he asked.

'No, I've had enough. I can't take any more mental torture. I'm not coming back – that's it.'

I could just about cope with the physical side of our turbulent marriage but the daily bullying, control and manipulation was too much to bear. The utter perversion of everything I did, everything he did, with our involvement in the sex industry woke me up. I could not stay.

Steve did his usual. He cried. Promised he'd stop drinking. Begged me to come home. Warned me I'd never survive without him, insisted I was nothing without him. But when I finally convinced him I would never change my mind, his level-headed reaction left me stunned. It shocked me far more than if he'd screamed that I was a worthless dirty whore in the foul language he always used with me.

'Right, Dee. I get it – but what about the boys? You know you'll break their hearts.'

To cause as little disruption as possible in Bret and Brad Lee's young lives, I told Steve they could stay with him and keep going to the same school until I found a place to rent. He agreed and, in a move that left me open-mouthed with shock, he even said he would hand over birth certificates and passports for me and the boys so I had everything I needed to help us secure a home.

I knew that, as soon as I had somewhere to live, the boys would stay with me and never go back to their father. But in the meantime I was desperate to see them.

'Well, you know where we live,' said Steve.

'No, I'm not coming back to that house. Ever. I'll only see you where there are people around us.'

We agreed to meet on Wednesday at the West Bromwich branch of McDonald's, halfway between his house at Great Barr in Birmingham and Tanya's flat. I could stomach seeing

Steve if it meant I could be with my boys; I couldn't stand being without them.

Until then I busied myself looking through local newspapers to find a job and a flat. I was ready to do anything except sell myself. I'd scrub loos, wash floors, clean windows – anything. Prostitution had not been my choice and now I was in charge of my future I would never turn tricks again.

I would do whatever it took, within respectable reason, to support me and my boys but would not go on benefits. I had always been a grafter and the thought of getting money without working for it first, while I was fit and healthy, did not sit well with me. Claiming benefits would have made my life easier and paved the way to finding a place to stay far sooner, but I wanted to regain self-respect and reclaim my personal power as much as I wanted a flat for my sons and me. Regardless of everything I'd been through, I was still proud. If I'd gone to social services, Steve would have pointed and laughed at me for being a sponging failure.

'Ha! There she is with a begging bowl. See! She's nothing without me.'

So I made enquiries about cleaning and telesales jobs. And I booked a Thursday appointment with the Citizens Advice Bureau for guidance on how to get a divorce and full custody of my kids.

Those few days at Tanya's flat were emotional. I was excited to know I really had escaped Steve's grip but sad because I missed the boys. I was nervous because I had no clue what I'd end up doing for a living to support the three of us, yet positive about my life ahead. It certainly could not get any worse and I would work tirelessly to make it better.

I spoke to Bret and Brad Lee a lot on the phone. Each call was the highlight of my day.

'When are you coming home, Mummy?' asked Bret.

'Darling, Mummy isn't coming back to that house. I'm looking for a new place to stay – just me, you and Brad Lee. Won't that be nice?'

'Yaay! Will we have a new bedroom?'

'Yes, my love. You and Brad Lee can have whatever you like when everything's sorted out.'

Brad Lee was ecstatic when I told him I'd booked tickets to see the *Goldilocks* pantomime at the weekend.

'Yesss! Can we buy lots of sweets?'

'Absolutely – but only if you share them with me!'

I loved hearing the boys so happy but my heart always sank when Steve took the phone.

'You're definitely not coming back then?' he said.

'No way, Steve! Our marriage is dead and has been for years. That's it for good this time. I'm seeing a lawyer soon. It's over.'

Finally I was the one in control. At last I had the upper hand. And in a few days, once I had Bret and Brad Lee back, we would start a happy new life together.

Just my boys and me.

Chapter 14
Bret. Brad Lee. Steve. No!

I arrived at McDonald's bang on time at 6pm to find Bret and Brad Lee waiting outside with Steve. They ran over and flung themselves at me as soon as they saw me.

'Mummy! We've missed you millions and billions!'

'I've missed you like mad, too! I love you so, *so* much!'

What a feeling. Stooping down to their height, wrapping my arms around them both and pulling them in tight. Kissing their soft curls, stroking the skin on their beaming faces, inhaling the smell of my beautiful boys. Mum and sons, best friends, together again. A reunion after years apart could not have been warmer.

Then they were scalded by the wrath of their dad. Steve looked furious and stormed over to chide the boys. 'What have I told you two about running off?'

Inside McDonald's, Bret and Brad Lee both wanted to sit next to me, as always. They plonked themselves either side of me and shuffled their seats up so they could be as close as possible without actually sitting on my knee. I'd always liked to dress them the same and right then, in their matching yellow and blue fleece tops, they looked super-cute and felt extra-cuddly.

The boys barely glanced at Steve sitting opposite but they knew he was there, scrutinising their slightest move. I hated Steve's strict disciplinary methods but was grateful that he only ever raised his fists to me, never them. It made them very well-behaved boys but it also made them mummy's boys.

'I love you to pieces, Mummy,' said Bret. 'I missed you so much.'

'I love you EVEN more than you love me,' said Brad Lee.

'That's impossible,' I said. 'Because I love you both more than all the love in the whole world.'

Steve stared straight ahead. My boys and I were forever saying how much we loved each other and he would always silently seethe through our gushy proclamations. In all our time together Steve never said he loved me. Not once.

For the next hour, between mouthfuls of Happy Meal fries and Chicken McNuggets, the boys' chatter was quieter than usual. I knew that meant Steve had been snapping at them, darkening their bright natures that shone when they were with me.

'Has Daddy told you that he and Mummy aren't going to live together anymore?'

The boys' eyes widened.

'It doesn't mean we don't love you two, just because me and Dad don't want to live together. Doesn't mean we don't want to be with you. Mummy is just having a few days away to sort out a brand-new house for us.'

Usually I can't stand the cheap toys in Happy Meals, the daft little plastic things that are played with for an hour then discarded. But at that moment I was grateful that those toys distracted Bret and Brad Lee from the news I was breaking.

I didn't want to take my eyes away from my sons to look at Steve, didn't want to miss a second's sight of them, but I didn't want Bret and Brad Lee to sense the horrible atmosphere that would have spoiled their tea out on a school night.

When I did take in Steve, he looked strange – really odd. I'd seen him stare at me with hatred before many times and, lately, all the time. But now, as he sat there not eating anything, he glared through me with an even more ferocious level of anger; it was a sinister look I hadn't seen before.

With tea over, wrappers scrunched and binned, Bret and Brad Lee proudly stuck out their tummies to show me how full they were. The evening neared the boys' bedtime and soon it was time to go.

'Do you want a lift to your friend's house?' asked Steve.

But I knew Steve's ways all too well. I'd never have let him near Tanya's flat, never have revealed my hiding place – he'd have terrorised me there.

'No, no. My tram stop's just over the road,' I said.

'Well, at least sit in the car and have a few more minutes with Bret and Brad Lee.'

Since it meant more precious time with my boys, I buckled my giggling sons into their booster seats at the back of Steve's

Daihatsu and climbed into the passenger seat. I flashed back to the first time I was in this car, aged only 16. I was infatuated with Steve then. His tight curly hair had reminded me of my real dad. His denim jacket and big gold rings backed up his boasts about being wealthy enough to look after me. His aftershave made me delirious with passion.

Now, sitting next to him in the same car and smelling the scent that signified a decade of abuse, I felt sick. So many lies, broken promises, attacks. The only good things to come from our volatile union were Bret and Brad Lee. Through years of hell at his hands, I'd bolstered myself to put up with anything for the sake of our boys.

'Do you want a fag?'

I didn't smoke, except for rare occasions when Steve insisted I had a fag with him but never in front of my boys. But I knew Steve's temper was simmering so I took a cigarette to keep the peace. Steve chain-smoked one after the other and refused to open a window even as the car filled with a thick fog. He was acting strangely, even for him.

I knew I had to get out before he flipped. I clicked open the passenger door and turned my face over my right shoulder to look back at Bret and Brad Lee, who were still playing with their Happy Meal toys.

'Only three more sleeps until I take you to see *Goldilocks* at the theatre! We can get ice-cream tubs and sweets if you like.'

'Can't wait, Mummy! Love you to pieces. See you soon.'

Their excitement was infectious and I was looking forward to the pantomime as much as they were.

'Mummy's got to go now.'

As I turned back to face the front and open the car door, Steve grabbed me in a headlock. He pulled me until I was sprawled out across the front seats with my head in his lap.

'Shut the fucking door, I'm going to kill you! I've got a knife in the car and I'm going to use it.'

His fist pounded my face, his rings sliced into my skin over and over again. The force of his punches made a crunching sound against my cheekbone, jaw, ear and eye socket.

'Mummy! Mummy, are you OK?'

'Daddy! Stop it! Stop hurting Mummy!'

My boys. My boys should not see this.

I slammed my hand on to the steering wheel horn and the noise made Steve loosen his grip. Kicking the passenger door open, I tumbled out on to the icy road. Disoriented and dizzy, I lay crumpled in a heap on the ground. In all Steve's beatings, this was the only one to make me see stars.

The engine revved, tyres screeched and Steve's car lurched straight at me. I scrambled to the kerb and scraped my body under a metal barrier surrounding the new bus station. I knew Steve would not stop until he'd run me over; he detested me that much. I knew, from bleak experience, that he had no off switch, no limits when it came to brutality against me.

The car swerved, jerked and then stopped. The passenger window rolled down. Steve pointed at me cowering on the pavement, laughed and sarcastically said, 'Are you all right?' When the window rolled back up, Steve was still laughing as he sped off without his headlights on. It was a crazy, psychotic laugh, an ominous 'heh, heh, heh'. I'd never heard it before – I still hear it to this day.

Distraught, humiliated, enraged, I staggered a few yards to my tram stop with the cold sting of February biting at my face. It was 7.20pm. Thankfully, my tram arrived immediately.

'Oh my God – can I get you an ambulance? Sit down, love. What's happened?' The tram conductor's reaction told me my injuries were, once again, shocking. He let me borrow his phone as there was no credit on mine.

I know now that I should have called 999 or run to the police station. For years my life has been full of 'what ifs?' What if I'd known then what Steve would do? I would have stayed in the car, gone back to the house, stayed with him forever despite the kickings and knifings. Let him do anything to me, scratch my eyes out, anything. But for some reason, maybe because I needed comfort from a friend without having to explain my merciless husband, I called Tanya.

'He's battered me.'

She gasped. 'You are effing joking? Come here, come back here now.'

Adrenaline and white fury blocked the physical pain. I didn't know I was cut until I saw blood dripping from my face on to my coat.

But I would not be a victim; I would not let Steve win. After Tanya's house I'd go to the police station, still bloodied, to show them what an evil bastard he really was. It wasn't the harshest of the hundreds of attacks I'd endured from him but it would be the last – I'd make sure of that.

Tanya was waiting for me at her door. As soon as I stepped into the warmth of her flat, only 10 minutes after throwing myself from Steve's car, my phone rang. Steve's name flashed on to the screen, juxtaposed with the cheery beeps of the Nokia ringtone.

Hands trembling, I lifted it to my bleeding ear. I could hear Steve breathing in a deep, heavy, stressed way. In a half whisper, he spoke 10 words before cutting me off.

'I've killed the kids. Now I'm going to kill myself.'

I couldn't hear the boys in the background. I could always hear them chattering or laughing whenever Steve called but I couldn't hear them: I heard nothing.

Tanya came with me to Bilston police station, which was alarmingly busy. All the staff seemed hurried, darting around, radios clicking and crackling with sharp, fast conversations.

'Bet they won't have time for a domestic,' I thought. The police had been to our home many times when neighbours reported my screams as my husband smashed me around the place. Officers would separate us into different rooms and try to persuade me to make a statement. Even when I did, Steve used his well-honed manipulative skills to get me to drop the charges. I worried the police would lose patience with me after so many call-outs but when I ran straight to the enquiries desk the officer looked genuinely concerned.

'It's my husband – he says he's killed my children,' I cried, tears mixing with the blood on my face.

'Did he do that to your face?' he asked.

'Please, it doesn't matter about me. Just find my boys, please? God, please find my boys!'

The officer didn't look at me when he made a brief phone call. Then he came from behind the counter and said, 'We need to take you to West Bromwich police station. They can help you there.'

I remember nothing of driving there in a police car – I don't even know if it was a blue-light journey. When I arrived at the bigger station Tanya and I were taken to the family room. A sergeant came to see me and asked, urgently yet sensitively, if I knew of Steve's whereabouts.

'I can't get through to him,' I sobbed. 'He's turned his mobile off. But he has my sons and says he's killed them.'

'Mrs Wilson, please, do you have any idea where he could be?'

I had no idea. I gave them our home address, Steve's mobile number, his car registration, all the details I could but I couldn't give them the vital clue they needed about where he'd gone.

The sergeant left Tanya and me alone in the family room. With its blue sofa, pot plant on the window-sill, box of toys in the corner and magazines on the coffee table, it was designed to feel homely. The framed beach watercolour was supposed to have a calming effect, which is difficult to achieve by the very fact you're there at the police station.

Tanya kept squeezing my hand, hugging me tightly and saying, 'You'll be all right. No father would do anything terrible to his own kids.'

The wall-mounted television showed a documentary about the Moors Murderers. Black-and-white pictures of grinning young children who never grew old flashed up. Stills of Ian Brady and Myra Hindley came on to the screen. Both had the dead eyes and cold stare I had seen earlier that evening.

As torturous hours passed I calmed down. Steve wouldn't do that to our boys. He'd never hit them, he'd never harm them. It was me he despised, not our sons. He'd wanted to give me an almighty fright and it had worked. He needed to pull a big stunt to jolt me out of my decision to leave. This would blow over but he'd ruined all chances of the boys ever living with him. Maybe I'd still have the new start, the happy new life. Maybe this was the last attempt he'd ever make to terrify me back to him. At 26, I was strong and I was determined life would be better from now on. Steve had totally blown it with me and the boys now.

Was that a helicopter buzzing overhead?

The agonising time dragged, my racing mind slowed and my body gave in to exhaustion. My swollen and skinned face began to throb. Tanya was holding my hand and doing a good job of convincing me my kids would be OK. I hadn't realised I'd twisted a tissue into tiny pieces until I saw the pile of Kleenex confetti by my feet.

It was 10pm by the time the sergeant returned. Officers had stuck their heads around the door every half-hour or so, asking if we were OK, if we needed anything and offering cups of tea. But this time the sergeant was accompanied by a female colleague and came over to the sofa. I glanced at Tanya, who looked white and didn't meet my eyes. The sergeant knelt in front of me, held my hand and faced me straight on. I could see tears in his eyes.

'Denise, we have found the boys,' he said.

'Great! That's brilliant, that is. When are you bringing them here to play with the...'

The sergeant gently raised his hand to stop me mid-sentence.

'Denise,' he said, slowly shaking his head. 'I am *so* sorry. The boys are dead, we got there too late. They were dead. I am *so* sorry.'

Bret. Brad Lee. Steve. *NO!*

'He's really done that? He's really killed the kids? Bret and Brad Lee? *No!* He hasn't. Please say no?'

Numbness. Disbelief. Total shock. I knew it was real but I didn't want it to be.

Screaming inside or outside my head. *No, no, no!* Clenching my fists, my teeth. Screwing my eyes closed. *NO!* Agony in every part of my body, swinging back my arm and slapping the sergeant, blacking out...

Chapter 15

'I Said He Was A Bad 'Un. You Wouldn't Listen'

I awoke on the floor of the family room, a doctor standing over me. A female police officer was holding my hand.

'Denise, do you remember what happened?'

'My boys? Please tell me that didn't happen. I was only eating with them a couple of hours ago.'

'I am *so* sorry.'

'*NO!*'

I didn't want to speak to anyone. I did not want to hear them saying things like 'sorry for your loss'. I could not bear to open my eyes and see strangers' faces etched with concern. I didn't want to close my eyes and imagine the smiles of my sons if I could not see them again. I didn't feel anything but a hollowness inside that echoed with animalistic moans, which I wasn't sure were imagined or expressed.

'I am so sorry, Denise,' said the doctor. 'Is there anything I can give you?'

'Yes,' I replied, 'a lethal injection. I mean it. Please?'

And I really did mean it. Bret and Brad Lee were my reason for living and without them there was no need for me to be alive: they were my world. There could be no pain worse, nothing more hateful than existing right then. Dying would release me from a life I simply could not face and reunite me with the sons I couldn't live without.

Anger rankled and rose.

'Take me to Steve,' I told the sergeant.

'You know we can't do that.'

'Take me to him and I'll kill him. I'll do to him what he did to my boys.' I was screaming, sobbing, and determined to get to Steve.

'Denise, we will get you through this,' said the doctor.

The next thing I remember is waking up in a modern hotel room. The winter sun sliced through a chink in the curtains, gleaming like a blade.

Blade. My boys.

The sun that day wasn't a beautiful sight, it was cruel. How dare it shine on a day like this, when all the brightness and colour had been ripped away and would never return?

My bed sheets were so soaked with sweat they looked as if a bucket of water had been poured on to them. Tanya had stayed with me and said the doctor gave me sedative pills before the police brought us to the Howard Johnson Hotel. She'd sat up all night watching me. My sleep had been deep but so disturbed that I thrashed around in bed for hours.

There was a phone in the room but no one to call. The bed was puffed with a fluffy down-filled duvet that could never give me comfort. The service menu offered guests anything they wanted. But no one in the world could give me what I wanted. What I longed for urgently, physically: my boys back with me, holding them, feeling their warm cheeks against mine, hearing them laugh together. The ache was so acute it made my chest feel it was buckling, folding in half, closing tight.

That anguished, animal cry again.

'Denise, do you want a cup of tea?' Tanya asked.

But the only thing I wanted was my boys – to know what had happened to them, to see them. I turned on the television news hoping there would be no mention of Bret and Brad Lee, hoping this moment was not real and I was trapped in a hellish dream.

School pictures of Bret and Brad Lee on the screen, then a wooded area I did not recognise. Steve's green and silver Daihatsu. A big, strong-looking police officer handcuffed to a smaller man, whose head was covered by a blue blanket: Steve.

Things like that didn't happen to people like me. It just happened to folk on telly. And now my life was on telly.

I wanted alcohol, anything to blur the truth of the day and my life from then on. But I could not drink because I had to go to the police station to be interviewed. I had to bury Steve, had to tell officers every last disgusting, despicable detail about him.

The female officer who'd held my hand after I passed out came to the hotel to collect me. She was Amanda Harvey, a member of the CID, who had been assigned as my police liaison officer. Immediately it seemed she was on my side – an instant ally. Amanda explained that she would be there for me from then on, guiding me through the traumatic investigation and legal process ahead.

The two male interviewing officers were as sensitive as they could be but I had to answer questions about my entire 10 years with Steve in really important, long interviews just hours after I'd lost my kids. They wanted to know why I'd left, when I'd left, when all that mattered was that I'd lost my sons. I was so overcome, stressed and distraught that I was in physical pain; it was too much.

Amanda held my hand throughout. And when we went to the police canteen for dinner breaks she hugged me. I could never eat, just pick at things. Then it was back into the stark interview room, just with a desk and two officers behind it, for more questions.

At first they wouldn't tell me how Steve had killed Bret and Brad Lee. They didn't need to, I just knew. For years I'd lived with Steve's threats and boasts of how the SAS had taught him how to kill in seconds. 'You go for the main artery on the left side of the neck, the carotid artery, cut it and that's it. You're dead,' he'd say, sinking his fingers deep into the left side of my throat to show he could, and would, do it.

So I told the police. 'I know what that bastard did. He cut the left side of their necks, didn't he, the carotid artery? Didn't he?'

The officers gave away nothing but I had a dreadful feeling that I was right.

My instincts told me more details about my sons' murders than I wanted to know.

'He killed Brad Lee first, I know he did – he always said Bret was the weaker of his boys and knew he was squeamish. He would have wanted Bret to suffer by seeing his brother killed first.'

The officers didn't say I was right but their stunned expressions did.

Slowly, details of the nightmare were revealed. Every point, every sketchy fact I learned of my sons' killing felt like a hot iron searing into my brain.

Steve had phoned the police and told them he'd killed his kids, which is why the station was so frenetic when I arrived. He said he was in Bewdley, Worcestershire, then switched off his phone to foil attempts to track him.

In fact, he'd driven to a secluded spot behind a shed at a golf club in Handsworth, which was less than four miles from McDonald's. In the Daihatsu car he loved, he had stabbed the sons *I* loved. He used a craft knife blade taped to a beer mat to slash Brad Lee's throat, then killed him by stabbing a screwdriver into the wound. Then he turned on Bret, who was slain by his daddy plunging a screwdriver twice into his neck. There was evidence that Bret, my boy who could be scared witless by a stripy cat, had been sick.

A police helicopter had spotted Steve's car. When he saw paramedics arrive he stuck the screwdriver into his chest, which caused a superficial puncture wound. Typically, he'd been too much of a coward to snuff out his own evil life. He could only kill lovely, innocent little boys – his own boys. He hated me more than he loved them.

I know why Steve stayed alive: he wanted to see and hear my reaction to his depraved deed. That was his motive, the nub of his revenge. He wanted to know that he had succeeded in destroying and blackening my very soul.

Steve would have loved making that phone call to me, knowing before I did that he made my world implode. He would have enjoyed the police manhunt, relished the fact helicopters were scouring the land for him. His wickedness was such that he liked to create drama around him. He liked to set up fights, fallouts and conflict of all description. He liked attention even though it was negative attention. It made him feel important, manly, powerful. All eyes had to be on him.

He was under police guard at hospital and I wanted to get to him, tear his foul flesh to pieces. Rip his head off.

'Take me to see him. Let me do to him what he did to my kids. I'm begging you, please.'

'We can't do that, Denise. He's in police custody handcuffed to the bed – he won't get away with this.'

Police needed to know if Steve had owned a craft knife and kept one in the car – and could I point one out if I saw one in the shop? They needed to know what kind of screwdriver it was – and had he ever attacked anyone with one? It was hard to think clearly about any answers; hard to make sense of something so senseless.

I was bewildered. Why was I enduring days of intense questioning when Steve had admitted on tape that he had killed my boys? I felt as if I was on trial.

'It's just procedure,' said Amanda.

But on the second day of interviewing it soon became apparent that it was something more. Because as the officers' questions changed tack, I knew that Steve wouldn't surrender without a fight. He wouldn't go down without trying to haul me down with him.

Incredibly, Steve was making allegations about *me*.

The officer said, 'Steve tells us you got gangsters to kill the boys because you wanted money for drugs.'

It was astounding.

'I have never touched drugs in my life,' I said. 'Gangsters? What the hell is he talking about?'

It went on and on.

'Steve claims you have been working as a prostitute.'

'Yes, I have,' I said. 'But I had no idea what went on at Sensations until I got there. He forced me to work there.'

'Your husband said in his interview that he did not know you were sleeping with clients and that you told him you were only a receptionist.'

'Bullshit!'

Sometimes my answers were broken into pieces by sobs, sometimes I was in such a daze they came out in a robotic monotone. But always, always they were true: I had nothing to hide, had done nothing wrong. Not in the eyes of the law anyway. But I had left my boys with a man who had never been violent towards his kids, and I knew that man was a demon. It was the worst decision of my entire life. Guilt was building up and ready to hijack my grief but I couldn't even begin to grieve until I'd pushed myself through the police interviews.

I told no lies but knew that what I was telling the officers sounded far-fetched. I tried to describe how Steve had manipulated and brainwashed me to the point where if he had told me the grass was purple I'd have agreed. I tried to put into words why my immense fear and his extreme power was the reason for never progressing the full file of police complaints I'd made against my husband. I tried to explain how he and I lived in a steel bubble, how he was obsessive and possessive. Other than Stacey, Konrad and Gemma, no one else knew the horror of living under Steve's brutal rules and it was difficult convincing the police of a story that sounded like a horror fiction.

All the while I could hear screaming in my head, which sometimes sounded like me and sometimes sounded like Bret and Brad Lee. Whenever I blinked I saw my boys' lifeless and bloodied bodies. All I wanted to do was flee the room, see my sons, hold them, kiss them, warm them up; breathe life back into them. Maybe I could fix them, maybe Mummy could make it all better. Amanda told me they just looked like they were asleep. I would not, *could* not, believe Bret and Brad Lee were truly gone until I was able to see them for myself.

But I couldn't see my boys until their post-mortems had been carried out. I needed to be near them somehow, to feel their presence, so I asked if I could go to the scene where Steve had taken them. It took two days of constant police questioning until I was allowed.

The shops we passed in the car on the way there were full of Valentine's Day gifts. I asked Amanda if they'd stop the car and I got out and bought Bret and Brad Lee two big brown teddies with hearts on their tummies that said 'I love you'. I hugged them close as we drove and I cried into their soft fur.

Steve had taken my sons to an old factory unit hidden from Hill Top Golf Course by trees and a shed. He knew he'd have to find somewhere that provided coverage for the car; he knew a helicopter would be sent to find him. It was a strange place for my sons to lose their lives. I felt cold standing there. Empty. And I cried and cried.

Bret and Brad Lee had loved their daddy's car. They had stuck their heads out of the windows one snowy Christmas Eve, yelling 'Merry Christmas!' and spreading cheer to the last-minute shoppers they passed in Walsall. They had stood on the side treads and clung on to the window bars while their daddy had driven along Brean Sands beach in Somerset, squealing with delight as they were soaked in sea spray yet all the way shouting at Steve, 'Go faster, Daddy! Faster!'

But in the end they lost their precious lives in their daddy's car here, behind the police tape, in this place devoid of beauty. I dared not imagine the horror, terror and betrayal on their little faces as their crazed dad stole the lives he helped create but did not deserve. I tried not to think about it but scenes of my beautiful boys, my angels, being stabbed by their devil dad kept pulsing before my eyes as if in a flickering horror film.

I couldn't stay away. The next day I asked to go back to the scene again. Until I could see my boys' bodies, I needed something, somewhere, to help me feel a sense of the two lives I'd brought into the world. But I wish I hadn't gone back: because I saw that the teddies I'd left there had been stolen.

After a couple of nights staying at the hotel near the police station, Tanya had to go home. She had tried her best to help me through something that was impossible to get through. She had done everything she could to help me cope. But it was hard for her too – a young woman in her early twenties cannot be expected to know what to say and do at a time like that. Truth is, no one can. Even the world's most eminent psychologists would fail. Because there was nothing in the entire world that could bring me comfort even for one second.

I couldn't hack staying in the hotel on my own because of my horrific nightmares. There was absolutely no way I could go back to the house, where I'd see my boys' clothes, toys, beds. Amanda had even gone to Dorothy Perkins to buy me a fresh top and trousers because I had no clean clothes and could not stomach going back to Linden Avenue.

There was nowhere else for me to go, I had no choice. So, when my mum called the police to ask if I was OK, they asked if I could stay with her.

I'd barely seen or spoken to Mum in the decade since she disowned me for moving in with Steve. And I will never, *ever* forget her words when I turned up at her door.

'Told you what he was like, didn't I? I said he was a bad 'un. You wouldn't listen, would you?'

Chapter 16

Everyone Is Sorry.
No One More Than Me

I don't blame Mum, I don't judge her and I don't resent her. She had a lot of Dave's ways. And I, more than anyone, know what it's like to be bullied and brainwashed by a man.

Mum might not have said the right things at the right time to me, and she might have had to ask Dave's permission before she allowed me to come back home. But she was there for me.

When she talks about Bret and Brad Lee, she weeps and bitterly regrets not being part of their lives. I know exactly how she heard what happened and how much their deaths hurt her because she relives it often and cries each time.

The day after Steve killed Bret and Brad Lee, police knocked on Mum's door at 6am. They asked if there were any children in the house because they just wanted to speak to adults. My sister Nicky never left home. She had a son, Benjamin, just before Brad Lee was born and because Nicky wasn't in a lasting relationship with Ben's dad she and her son lived there with Mum and Dave. Benjamin was sleeping in the back room so police asked Mum, Dave and Nicky to sit down, then they broke the news.

'It's about your grandkids, Bret and Brad Lee Wilson. I'm sorry to tell you they have been killed.'

They assured Mum I was fine and being looked after by a liaison officer. But a day later she read in the paper that I was 'being comforted by family' and rang the police, saying, '*We* are her family. She should be with us.'

So I was back in my childhood home and sharing a room with my sister Nicky again. But I didn't want to be there, or anywhere that wasn't with my boys. I had to see them. I didn't want to wait until they'd been cleaned up; I just wanted to be with them.

After three days the police finally let me see Bret and Brad Lee at the Coroner's Court. Mum and Amanda came too. I could see my sons only through glass but desperately wanted to touch them, pick them up and cuddle them until they were alive again.

My gorgeous boys were lying there on a trolley, covered up to their necks in red velvet-silk blankets that looked like something Snow White wore in one of the Disney DVDs we'd watched on our duvet movie nights. Brad Lee looked peaceful. Asleep. But when I saw Bret, I lost it. His beautiful face was bruised; he had cuts to his cheeks and lip. That broke me.

'I knew it! Look what that bastard's done to Bret! He's beaten my baby up,' I told Mum, who was already crying.

I knew for sure then that Bret had struggled to get out of the car and Steve had hit him. I knew what my poor boy must have been through.

Steve had demanded a second post-mortem to prolong my agony. It was his right as a defendant to ask for a second one and he would have done it for no other reason than to hurt me. But after a few more long, agonising days, my sons were moved to Henley's funeral home near Mum's house in Oldbury, West Midlands. The staff were so nice to me there, and I was there a lot – from nine to five most days, sometimes longer. They should have finished work at five but often stayed until 8pm just to let me have the time with my boys. I could have spent my life there.

Bret and Brad Lee's coffins were laid beside each other with a chair between them, where I sat for hours, holding their hands. Their little hands were so white, so cold. They felt like glass.

The staff told me I could play them music if I liked, and because they loved karaoke I brought in their favourite Westlife CD. I talked to them about happy things we had done, cried about the things we could never do. And all the time I told them how much Mummy loved them. How sorry I was for not protecting them.

'Sorry, boys, I am so sorry. I should have been there for you. Best friends forever. I should have protected you from him.'

I would have given anything, *anything*, just to hold them one more time. Just to hear them speak, for them to be awake again even for five minutes.

When you wish for something so desperately, when you are so broken and so utterly wrung out, your mind torments you.

Because I'd have sworn I heard Bret and Brad Lee breathing. I was convinced I saw those red silk shrouds rise up and fall as they inhaled and exhaled.

I alerted the funeral staff. 'Look! Come quick! I saw their chests move – I think they're alive.'

'Denise, listen, love, I'm afraid that's just natural gasses leaving their bodies. I really am sorry.'

Once again, mired in terrible circumstances, I became aware of other people's kindness. The funeral parlour staff knew the boys supported Aston Villa so they wrote to the club, which sent a framed, signed shirt. They even contacted Westlife, who sent signed photographs which we tucked inside their coffins. A friend gave me St Christopher necklaces to keep the boys safe on their final journey. And a neighbour gave me the 10 pences she'd saved 'so the boys could spend it on the other side'.

I know they have to refrigerate bodies at funeral parlours, so every night at 10pm one of the funeral home staff called me. 'Denise, that's the boys going to bed now. Goodnight.'

When the funeral director gently asked if I wanted the boys buried or cremated, my answer was resolute.

'If you bury my sons, I will be arrested because I'll jump into their graves,' I said. I'd have thrown myself on top of their coffins and told them I was still there for them, regardless. I would have cracked up, dug them up. I had visions of police dragging me away from the graves and me ending up in the psychiatric ward. 'It has to be cremation.'

When he asked if they could wash my boys, I didn't need time to think.

'No,' I said. 'I am their mum and I will do that. That's my job.'

It was my last task as a mother. I was proud that Bret and Brad Lee were always immaculate and would make sure they would go to the other side just so. It was up to me to tend to them, to look after their every need.

The staff led me into a room where they'd laid Bret and Brad Lee on a metal grid table with a drain underneath. Mum said she'd help. My boys had looked like porcelain dolls when they were laid out in the funeral home but now I saw the savage truth about what my little ones had endured. I saw the screwdriver marks down their chests, the stabbing wounds at their throats which had desecrated their perfect bodies, stolen their priceless lives.

If I'd known that seeing them like that, washing them like that, would haunt me for years, I'd never have done it. If I'd known I'd hallucinate about their pale, limp, bare bodies. But I was immersed in grief, crazed with guilt. I was in shock and flooded with so many emotions I felt none. I was a zombie.

So Mum and I used a shower head to wash my dead sons' grey bodies and shampoo their lovely dark hair. While I set about getting Brad Lee ready, Mum really struggled to wash Bret.

'Dee, I can't do this – I'm afraid I'm going to break his little arm.'

'Don't worry, Mum – please carry on. He's not going to feel it now. Come on, we can do this.'

In the end I took over from Mum.

I was advised to choose loose clothes for my boys because their bodies had started to become rigid. They said it was best to dress them in high necks because of the injuries. So I picked navy-blue fleece jackets and their favourite blue tracksuit bottoms with press studs down the side. They wore their newest trainers, which they'd insisted had made them run faster. I knew they wouldn't need trainers where they were going but you have to do these things properly, don't you?

I'd had to go back to Linden Avenue to get their clothes and that was awful. Mum and Amanda were with me. It was eerily quiet but in my head I heard the echo of Steve's threats and in the background the sweet sound of Bret and Brad Lee's infectious laughter. Everything was familiar yet alien now life had changed so much. The picture of Steve and Trish's wedding was still on top of the telly. The boys' schoolbags, which were red with pictures of black footballs, were in the cupboard under the stairs because they always hung them up once they came in from school. But they would never bound in again, never curl up next to me on the sofa for a double cuddle.

Day-to-day mundane objects suddenly became precious treasures now that they belonged to little boys who were no longer here. Bret's school jotter with an unfinished story about playing football; Brad Lee's *Fireman Sam* book with the corner of a page folded. Scuffed and muddy shoes; their pillows that smelled of the apple shampoo they loved.

For a while I liked being there, standing in their bedroom, because I could feel my boys. But then I revisited the moment I saw them sleeping soundly in their beds with their drunken father unconscious between them. Then I relived that decision to turn away and leave them. A sense of their father's violence overwhelmed me and I had to leave the house immediately.

I knew there were things that had to be done. I understood that I had to be the one to arrange the boys' funeral and be available to speak to the police whenever they needed me.

But in between times during those purgatory days, between the boys' deaths and their funerals when they were here yet not here, I drank. Whisky, straight, from a teacup. I sank a 75cl bottle on my own every day. On my first night back at Mum's house, I emptied the drinks cabinet of Bacardi, vodka and beer. I was wrecked. I smoked my head off, too. When I offered Mum a fag she asked, 'How long have you been smoking?'

'Two or three days.'

When I tipped my handbag out on to the kitchen table, six packets of cigarettes fell out. I was a complete mess. And I didn't care because I had no purpose. I was Bret and Brad Lee's mum but they weren't alive anymore – so was I a mother anymore? When you lose a husband, you are a widow. When you lose parents, you are an orphan. But when you lose your kids, who are you? No one. I was no use to anyone.

I didn't want to just numb the pain, I wanted to obliterate it. So I drank to the point of losing all my senses. I'd fall asleep for a couple of hours and start drinking again when I woke. Sometimes Mum joined me – she knew she drank too much. Other times Nicky sat with me and she really was a rock.

I have a hazy recollection of hanging my head out of Nicky's bedroom window to be sick into the garden. I felt sure I'd drunk enough to end it all.

'I'm dying, Nicky – I really feel like I'm dying. Please give my boys a good funeral. I want them to have a horse-drawn carriage and be together.'

'You need to stop this, Dee,' said Nicky, crying. 'You need to be at the funeral. You have to gather all your strength together. You're a good girl but you're killing yourself.'

The police offered me counselling, which I declined, because in a way Amanda was better than any counsellor could have been. Whenever Mum was worried about me she called Amanda who would arrive in less than half an hour, no matter what time of night. When I wouldn't, *couldn't*, eat anything Mum sobbed at the sight of every one of her untouched meals. It was Amanda she called when my weight plummeted below seven stone.

Dave coped as best he could. Rather than show me gentle sympathy, he put all his energies into berating Steve; that was just his way. But he felt more than he could express because he went to see Bret and Brad Lee in the Chapel of Rest and came out crying. He helped me in the only way he knew how – by taking me to the pub.

Whenever the drink supplies ran out in Mum's house I grew scared of not being able to anaesthetise my thoughts. I'd have gone to the pub on my own and wept into endless tumblers of whisky but Dave warned me against it because the press were everywhere. Instead he took me to the pub with Mum and Nicky, and despite urging me to keep a low profile when we got there he'd tell everyone, 'This is the daughter whose kids have just been murdered.'

If I broke down in public, Amanda seemed to magically appear and drove me home. She even dealt with the press for me. My way of coping was to trawl through every single newspaper every day, analysing each word of the report in case I spotted any of Steve's lies. I had a desperate need to know everything about what had happened to Bret and Brad Lee because I worried police might be keeping things from me. Reading about my boys' murders helped me understand that it was real, it had really happened. But sometimes I read something that sent me into a furious rage or an endlessly sobbing state.

The *Sun*'s headline read: 'BIG MAC WITH DAD THEN BLOODBATH'. Bloodbath? Police had insisted the boys looked like they were sleeping in the back of Steve's car but this claimed something far worse. That really set me back.

Amanda was furious and contacted the *Sun* about the pain it had caused me. They were quick to offer an unreserved apology.

Everywhere I went people kept saying 'I'm sorry'. Even my poor mum. She kept a German Shepherd dog who was so bad-tempered we all called him Nasty Jake. One night, I was so drunk I let Nasty Jake into the kitchen and fed him pork scratchings but he turned on me and bit me really hard on the hand.

I remember falling to the floor and saying, 'I'm fine' before passing out. When I came round, Mum said, 'Oh, God, I'm so sorry – as if you haven't been through enough.'

Then there was the day I vomited while doing Mum's dishes. I spotted a screwdriver on the window ledge and it made me visualise my boys' terrible deaths.

'I'm really sorry, Dee, I should have thought. I should have moved it. Sorry.'

Everyone was sorry for so many things. But no one could ever be as sorry as I was.

Chapter 17
The Saddest Day

People always say, 'Why didn't you leave Steve years ago?' And I say, 'If I did, I'd have buried smaller coffins.'

Just before the boys' funerals, heartbreakingly too late, I saw that Bret and Brad Lee's murders had a horrifying inevitability. Steve wanted to destroy anything that was mine. He got rid of my friends, shut out my family. He took my youth by making me a stepmum at 16. And he stole my freedom by keeping tight control of all finances. But when Bret and Brad Lee were born I had maternal love that he could not break or take. The boys kept me going and gave me happiness, even when he battered me to a pulp. Even when he stamped all over my personal pride and dignity by forcing me into prostitution.

By then the only thing I had left was the kids. Nothing could hurt me if I had them. If he took them he knew I'd crumble and die inside, even if I didn't kill myself. I could see now that he resented the love Bret, Brad Lee and I shared. He would say, 'Why do you need to spend so much time with the boys? What about me?' Sick, twisted psycho.

Back then the shock of losing my boys was paralysing. And because it didn't seem real, because my mind couldn't take in the enormity of it, I had clear thoughts about what I wanted for their funeral. I knew, just as acutely, what I didn't want. And I told the vicar as much as soon as he arrived at Mum's house.

'Please don't come in here preaching about God. You and I both know that there is no God, because God would not have let this happen.'

The vicar was kind. 'I would never preach to you, Denise. I'm just here to go over what you'd like for your boys' service. Whatever you would like for your boys, we can do. You don't even need to mention God.'

I knew I wanted a very simple service because I couldn't have coped with anything more. 'Amazing Grace' was the only hymn I chose because I knew it meant forgiveness. I wanted to ask my boys if they could please forgive me for having to organise their funeral rather than the many more birthday parties they should have enjoyed.

Most of all I wanted my boys side by side, and I wanted a horse-drawn carriage for them because they loved horses. But the funeral directors in the area didn't have a carriage wide enough for two coffins. I was so adamant that Bret and Brad Lee would be together in death as they had been throughout their short lives that a bigger carriage was brought up from London. I appreciated that so much.

The carriage would leave from Linden Avenue because most of Bret and Brad Lee's friends lived nearby and wanted to follow the hearse. So Mum and I got to the house early to tidy up and make pots of tea before friends and relatives arrived. Mum said I would be expected to lay on drinks and I worried about being able to afford it but when I got to the house I found an envelope at the foot of the door. Inside was a sympathy card and £180 cash 'from all at Sensations'. I appreciated that too.

The house was a state because police had searched it and I suppose they can't be expected to put everything away afterwards. Bret and Brad Lee hadn't left it like that.

An elderly couple I hadn't seen before were the first to turn up. The lady came over to me and said, 'I am Steve's mum. I am ever so sorry.'

That was a shock.

She looked a bit like Margaret Thatcher because she wore a stern look and a smart suit. Steve's dad looked like a lovely man – the type of granddad who would have rolled around on the floor with Bret and Brad Lee, the grandkids he would never meet. The grandsons killed by his son. He looked terrified.

I had difficulty finding words for them. And I was scared to open my mouth in case I let rip with rage. So Steve's mum did most of the talking. She said Steve had been 'a bastard' from the age of three when he threw a kettle at her. In adulthood they'd won a court injunction to keep him away from them after he smashed the windows in their house – all because he hadn't been invited to a party there. She had, until only a few years previously, lived just down the street from us. She hadn't known Bret and Brad Lee had been born until she'd heard they died.

To be honest, I couldn't feel much for Steve's mum then. His family were all there but stayed over to one side of the room. My family didn't mix too much with them – we were too angry.

Amanda had contacted Konrad and Stacey to tell them of the funeral plans. By now both lived away and neither had any contact with me or Steve, but the police had ways of finding people. Officers broke the news that their dad had killed their little brothers before the news went live on television. I'd asked Konrad to choose four men from his side of the family to carry one of the coffins. I paid for two funeral cars – one for my family and one for Steve's. I hated Steve intensely but even then I knew it wasn't right to take it out on his family. Stacey arrived but didn't say much.

I had to work hard to restrain myself, to keep it together. This was my boys' final day yet I was going around my living room saying, 'Anyone like a cup of tea?' All the time I was thinking, 'What the hell is this all about?' People were chatting and I wanted to scream, 'This isn't a party, it's the saddest day of my life. My sons and my life have been torn to shreds and you think it's OK to stand around swapping small talk?'

Nicky squeezed my arm. 'Dee, the hearse is coming up the road.'

When I saw the black horses with their black feather plumes, my world shattered. The sound of horses clip-clopping up the narrow road, which was lined with cars parked all the way up to the canal bank, silenced everyone in the house and outside.

When the carriage pulled up, carrying two small white coffins and wreaths spelling out Bret and Brad Lee in red and white carnations, everything seemed wrong, real and final.

This was it, my boys' last journey. I knew I was never going to be able to be this close to them again. I fell to pieces.

'I can't do this!'

Dennis, the funeral director, put his arms around me. I felt it was more than a coincidence that he had the same name as my real dad because he showed me the warmth and understanding I always believed my dad would have given me.

He said, 'Come on, Denise – it's going to be all right and you are going to be strong. You will get through this, you will do your boys proud.'

Mum and Amanda held hands with me in the car and held me up when we got to the crematorium. It was packed out. Flowers from well-wishers lined the path. Photographers leaned over the railings. Hundreds of people waited outside to hear the service through speakers. Lots of friends I hadn't seen in years had turned up and Tanya was there. But I preferred to stay within the circle of my sisters, Mum and Amanda.

When we sat down inside, Nicky was great. She kept whispering kind words into my ear to help me cope. 'At least the boys aren't feeling any pain now, Dee. They're in Heaven now and they're smiling down to see their mummy being so brave today.'

My sister Angie didn't attend the boys' funeral. She was in a volatile relationship then and wasn't allowed to come. I did not have the headspace to think about the dark irony of that.

Amanda helped me choose some of the music for the service. We played Westlife and Mariah Carey's version of the Phil Collins song 'Against All Odds' because of the lyrics – there was an empty space in my heart and in my life and, against all odds, it was what I had to face.

That's exactly how I felt. I knew it wouldn't happen, but all I wanted was to hear a coffin lid knock. I know it would have freaked some people out but I'd have loved it. I'd have been thrilled to live a real version of the *Ghost* movie when Patrick Swayze dies but comes back for Demi Moore.

I'd written a speech about Bret and Brad Lee but when I stood up to read it in front of everyone I broke down after just a few lines. Amanda came up to the microphone and hugged me. That helped me gather the strength to carry on reading to the end.

Each member of my family laid a red rose on Bret and Brad Lee's little coffins. The last song was Bryan Adams' 'Everything I Do'. That wasn't quite Bret and Brad Lee's favourite song. What they loved singing most into the karaoke machine in the pool room was Boyzone's version of 'Father And Son'. They'd sung it with such sweet voices then but the lyrics were starkly inappropriate now.

When the coffins slowly disappeared behind the curtain, I tried to remember the advice from Dennis about staying strong but I couldn't do it. My legs turned to jelly and buckled beneath me. I couldn't walk away, *couldn't* leave my boys there, so I was the last to leave. I just sat there staring at the curtains. I wanted to stay there, in silence, in case I heard that knock on the coffin lid but it was hard to stop crying long enough to hear silence.

Outside Mum looked at the flowers and said to the lady beside her, 'Aren't they beautiful? They were my grandkids – that bastard killed my grandkids.'

The woman next to her said, 'That bastard was my son.'

Mum hadn't realised she was standing beside Steve's mother. What a terrible situation for them both. But my mum couldn't hold back. 'I have no qualms in calling your son a bastard. You're not expecting sympathy from me?'

Nicky gently led Mum away and reminded her that this wasn't the time or the place. Steve's mum knew better than to retaliate and instead stood rooted to the spot, staring at the flowers.

One of Mum and Dave's friends ran a pub called The Oliver Cromwell and the landlord generously held the wake for no charge. Everyone there offered me a drink but I didn't want alcohol. I wanted to feel every moment of my sons' last goodbyes.

If I'd had any booze, I might have said things, terrible things, that would have hurt a lot of people and I could never take back. I would have shouted at Steve's family, screamed at Dave. So to win the battle to control myself I accepted only glasses of Coke. This was my boys' day and I had to give them the best of me.

Bret and Brad Lee's school was closed to allow staff, parents and pupils to attend the funeral. The headteacher, Andy Leivers, told newspapers it was 'the saddest day in the school's history'.

Comfort came in people's memories of Bret and Brad Lee, in the stories I hadn't heard. The teachers who praised their hard work ethic, neat handwriting and many drawings and affectionate stories of their mummy. Their young friends who told of sunny afternoons playing football in the street and of envying Bret and Brad Lee because they had so many holidays and toy action figures.

A sea of faces passed mine, offering condolences and kind words. One man, Kevin Griffiths, did more than that.

He said, 'I know it's a stupid question to ask if you're all right but if ever you need anyone to talk to, ever need anything at all, promise to phone me.'

I'd seen Kevin at the club but we'd never spoken beyond a passing hello. Steve thought he was a friend but he forced himself on people by buying them drinks and barging into their snooker games. Kevin wrote his number on a scrap of paper, pressed it into my hand, gave me a really tight hug and a peck on the cheek then left.

The funeral directors' kindness continued long after the boys had been cremated. They promised that every Christmas they would leave flowers at the crematorium for Bret and Brad Lee. And sure enough they have. A friend told me that their framed pictures take pride of place in the family room at Henley's next to the Chapel of Rest. Dennis died soon afterwards. His staff told me no funeral had moved him more than the one he held for my boys.

Dennis had given me Bret and Brad Lee's last curls in a special envelope, which I keep alongside their first curls in a memory box. I sat for hours, looking at those tiny snippets of soft dark-brown hair, running them through my fingers but keeping them in a perfect curl.

They'd also made little ink imprints of the boys' hands. They looked so small. I wished I could hold their hands again. Dennis printed a lovely little poem on the back.

Sometimes you get discouraged
Because I am so small
Always leaving handprints
On furniture and walls.

But every day I am growing
And will be big some day
And all those tiny handprints
Will surely fade away.

So here's a special handprint
Just so you can recall
Exactly how my fingers looked
When they were only small.

Reading the Book of Condolence given to me by the boys' school also helped me get through those early days after the funeral. Their classmates wrote such lovely letters and drew pictures of Bret and Brad Lee looking very similar and with big smiles. Some painted pictures of headstones bearing their names.

There were lots of notes from little boys saying they wished they could play football together again. And there were a good few notes from girls saying they loved them and remembered that they used to play 'boys catch girls'. That would have made my boys blush. Bret and Brad Lee had always really liked girls, the little heartbreakers. It struck me that I would never meet the girlfriends they would bring home, never know if they'd have married or had kids of their own.

The messages from kids, the simple words that had shaky writing and misspellings but real clarity of thought, gave me most consolation. No one speaks ill of the dead, but seeing such heartfelt words and lovely compliments from little children who only knew how to tell the truth really moved me. I read them so many times I knew the words by heart.

One letter was so lovely I had it laminated. It says 'bye bye' at the top.

Dear Bret and Brad,

We all miss you. Your mum was really upset at the funeral. All the reporters were there. Your mum had to were (sic) sunglasses. I was very upset. I was crying a lot.

My mum nearly started crying when I started to cry. Your mum bought flowers saying Bret and Brad. After the funeral there were lots more flowers. Some of (sic) the school and some of (sic) Denise. Some of the grownups and some of the seven children that came to the funeral. Your dad did not come. He wasn't allowed out of court. Your sister dyed her hair blonde. I wish I knew how many sisters you had – I could have asked you that in the time you were alive and going strong. Why did it have to happen to you? Why did your dad kill you? I bet you were wondering why I did not bring you any flowers. That is because I am going to bring some to your sweet little heart tomorrow. Bye bye little ones. x

Another:

Hey Brad Lee and Bret.

Hope you're happy with the girls and boys in Heaven. Your Mum hopes your (sic) happy now. She misses you and hopes you will wait for her. Your friends really miss you, you know it's true. When they have a frown they will think of you and a smile comes around. The corners turn on their little mouths and they have no doubt but to smile.

The teachers miss you – you made them laugh when they felt blue. You made them worry when you never turned up in class. I miss you and will see you soon. Take care. Miss you both very much. Bye.

And another:

Dear Bret,

I miss playing with you because you made me laugh. I miss your cute smile. When everyone found out we all started crying because not just I thought you were really nice, everybody did. We all really want you back. We couldn't stop crying. I miss your laugh and your cute face and even your ear piercing. Mr Leivers didn't tell us until the next day after you were killed. I feel sorry for you, Brad and your mum. Everyone kept on saying, to make us happy, that heaven is a better place than down here. Miss you always, lots of love, x

I had letters from strangers, simply addressed: 'Bret and Brad Lee's Mummy, West Midlands'. And some were sent to the police to be passed on to me.

One was from a lady who said she'd had her first baby at the age of 44 and couldn't believe I was such a young mum, having to deal with so much. She sympathised with my terrible time and said I was an incredible person. That was nice to hear, although I certainly didn't feel incredible. She enclosed a medal bearing a picture of the Virgin Mary, and, although I wasn't feeling very religious at the time, it was a kind gesture that brought comfort.

And then came a very special letter, sent to Linden Avenue and written one day after the boys' deaths. It said:

Dear Denise,

I have had to write to you on hearing the terrible news today concerning the boys. I know you were only thinking of your two boys when you ran away to the women's rescue house.

I am so sorry, Denise, I really don't know what to say to you. I would just like you to know that should you need me for anything please don't hesitate to get in touch. I still have in my purse the little note that Bret wrote to me. I have never forgotten you and often wondered how you and the boys were.

I will pray that God gives you the strength to get through this terrible time. Take care and God bless. Regards, the lady on the train to Llandudno xxx

Chapter 18
A Special Embrace

Two days after the funeral, I changed my name by deed poll. I wanted to cleanse myself of all connection to Steve so reverted to my maiden name of Williams. I also instructed a solicitor to start divorce proceedings while Steve was in custody awaiting trial. I destroyed every picture I had of that evil bastard by ripping them into tiny pieces and stamping on them.

People kept asking how I was coping and I told them I was fine. I said that because secretly I had a perfectly logical answer to everything: suicide.

My pain would end. I wouldn't be a problem to anyone. Best of all, I could be with my boys again.

My life was all about a future with Bret and Brad Lee, and since they'd been ripped away from me I had no future. I was no longer a mother. I had no home of my own, no job, nothing. I was useless, worthless, a nobody. Now there was no reason for me to be on the earth, I started planning how I would leave it.

I could overdose with pills and drink, which was easy and would spare my family the sight of blood. Or I could walk into the sea and keep on walking until I drowned – the boys had always loved the seaside. But on the afternoon when I picked up Mum from her cleaning job and seriously considered driving at full speed to smash into a wall I knew I had to get help.

Counselling had been pointless. Amanda arranged it for me and Dave drove me there. The therapist was an older man who seemed perfectly nice. His office was lined with books and was posh-looking but comfy. He sat me down and said, 'I don't know what you are going through. I can't even begin to imagine how you feel but I lost my teenage son in a car crash so have some insight into the sudden loss of a child.'

I stood up. 'I'm sorry, mate, no disrespect to you, but you couldn't possibly understand how I feel.' Then I walked out. I've never had a single session of counselling since.

Amanda was encouraging me to lay the first bricks in rebuilding my life. She liaised with the council to organise a new house for me at Perry Barr, near Aston Villa's ground. I moved a few small bits and bobs in, but didn't move in myself, not even for one night. I could not bear to be alone and preferred staying at Mum's house.

Meanwhile I was trapped in limbo. Bret and Brad Lee's funeral was over so I had no arrangements to keep me busy or distracted from my dark thoughts. I didn't know what to do with myself and had no structure to my torturously long days. The only task I had was to meet Konrad in a car park because he'd asked if I had anything of his mum's. I went back to Linden Avenue and got that horrible box full of Trish's things and her ashes to give to her son. I knew from friends that he was still working at the factory, but I didn't know where he was living and didn't ask. His dad had killed my sons and I wanted little to do with Steve's family. We didn't say a lot to each other.

'Are you all right, Denise? I'm so sorry about the boys,' said Konrad.

'I've got nothing to say to you,' I said. I was scared to start opening up – terrified of what might have come out. It was safer, kinder, to say nothing. I didn't mind if I never saw Konrad, Stacey or any of Steve's relatives again, because we shared only someone very evil in common.

I spent hours sifting through my life's decisions and turning them over in my head. I could answer none of the questions tumbling around. Why didn't I take the boys when I left? Why did Steve have so much hatred inside him? Most of all, how could a father kill his own children? How could a dad stab little boys that were his own flesh and blood? That was the question that troubled me, and everyone who heard about Bret and Brad Lee's death, the most. For most people, the idea of a father taking his own sons' lives was way beyond comprehension. But I'd never known a good, loving, non-aggressive father so I had no yardstick.

Did I provoke Steve into it? Was I really born evil, just as he always said? Was that what Geraldine had alluded to all those years back when she'd read my palm? Was I the catalyst for so much tragedy, violence and distress? And would the rest of my life see me ricochet from one destructive relationship to another?

My troubled mind didn't quieten in sleep for I was plagued with a vivid recurring nightmare. It always began the same way. I was standing at the edge of a big field surrounded by trees and with sheds in the distance. Then I'd see Steve's car at the far side of the field. I'd hear Bret and Brad Lee screaming from inside and would see through the car windows the silver glint of a weapon jerking up and down.

I'd shout, 'It's OK, darlings – Mummy's coming!' And I'd start running towards them. Running faster than I ever had in my life. But the ground beneath me wasn't a field; it was an escalator going backwards. The faster I ran, the farther away the escalator took me. But I kept on running, screaming, until I heard no more sounds coming from Steve's car.

I'd jolt awake and find my face wet with tears, my body drenched in sweat.

Sometimes I heard small details from Amanda about Steve and that would colour my entire day.

'He's trying to claim diminished responsibility, Denise,' she said. 'Psychologists are testing him.'

I flipped. 'He's going to do everything he can to try to get off. He's going to get off, isn't he? He's mad but not clinically insane. That's the most frightening thing – he is sane, but pure evil. He had planned to kill the boys to hurt me, not because he didn't know right from wrong. He's a manipulative bastard. Tell the shrink to speak to me.'

Amanda told me the odd bit of information she had about Steve. I was hugely relieved to hear that the psychologist saw through Steve's lies and pathetic play acting and paved the way for him to face a criminal trial for double murder.

After a few days in hospital with his superficial wounds, Steve was transferred to Winson Green prison on remand. I detest violence but rejoiced when Amanda told me a prisoner had called the police station from jail and said, 'Tell that big bastard who killed his kids that we know he's coming here and we're waiting.'

A prison guard who drank in the same pub as some of my neighbours sometimes shared news about Steve. I was happy when I heard that even the other inmates hated him so much they'd thrown boiling water over him and put excrement in his food. I snorted with derision when I heard he'd become a born again Christian.

In jail, anyone who has harmed a child is rightly considered the lowest of the low and I hoped his fellow inmates would make Steve suffer in every way possible. Apparently, his cell mate asked to be moved because Steve had a picture of his dead wife in a coffin on his cell wall, which his solicitor had given him after visiting Linden Avenue. By now gossip was rife about Steve so I desperately hoped the story of his having pictures of Bret and Brad Lee with their throats cut on his cell wall was false. Surely he wouldn't have been able to get hold of them? I know none of his family visited him in jail and he didn't have any friends.

Later, when Steve had been transferred to Blakenhurst prison, near Redditch in Worcestershire, he attempted suicide. Newspaper reports said he had slashed his throat and chest with a razor and stabbed himself with a spoon, losing up to four pints of blood. When medics found him, he was saying, 'I want to be with my kids.'

I was furious that he had professed to love the boys he had killed and had tried to get out of the trial. I wanted him to live to answer for his horrific crime but was pleased that he would be in pain and still have to face the court. Although, to me, there was no need to wait for the trial because there was no question he was guilty. Steve had confessed to nurses in hospital and admitted his crime to police in a 999 call from the scene. If they'd let me stab him to death, we'd have had justice and saved all the time and public money spent on the trial.

Even though he was locked away, Steve could still strike terror into my soul. One afternoon, after dropping Mum off at work, I glanced in my car mirror and saw a green Daihatsu Fourtrak with a silver roof right behind me. Panic gripped me and I stamped my foot on the accelerator and shot off, earning angry beeped horns from all directions.

Breathless, I ran into Mum's house, slammed the door, locked it and hid upstairs in Nicky's room.

I called Amanda. 'He's escaped. Steve was behind me in the car, I swear. I told you he'd come after me, didn't I? He's out there. You need to help me go abroad. Please help me!'

Amanda was calm. 'Denise, slow down. Steve is in prison. His car is impounded. There is absolutely no way on earth he can be out there. No way. You must have seen another car the same. It wasn't Steve.'

It took a while to settle my nerves after that, because, even when I'd accepted that I couldn't possibly have seen Steve, I was dismayed and remorseful about something bad I'd done.

'Amanda, I've done something terrible.'

'What?' she said, the shake in her calm voice betraying her alarm.

'I jumped a red light.'

Amanda gave a long sigh. 'Denise, don't worry about it. I think, in the scale of things, even the harshest traffic cop would understand.'

If I wasn't reminiscing about my boys or freaking out about Steve, I just felt lost. As if there was no place in the world I fitted in. If I went out I'd see other mums with their kids and feel resentful if they didn't look attentive enough to their little ones. Or I'd envy them so much for being lucky to have healthy kids I'd be consumed with jealousy. Why did they deserve to have children when I couldn't have mine?

All the time, wherever I was, I'd feel as if everyone was looking at me, whispering that I was the mum who had left her kids with their murderous father.

I knew I needed help but didn't know where to find it. So instead I stayed in – and drank.

A week after the funeral, while I was working my way through yet another bottle of whisky, Kevin Griffiths came to my mind from nowhere. I think it was his tight hug as he left the boys' wake. That embrace felt amazing. Special. It felt kind, genuine and warm. And it was the first time I'd felt that way since the boys died. I needed to talk to someone who wasn't family because I could see sharing my misery was exacerbating their own.

Until the day of the funeral Kevin and I had exchanged only a word or two and I felt our lack of connection meant I could have an open and honest chat. I called his mobile and simply said, 'I need someone to talk to.'

He said, 'I'll come to meet you straight away.' We arranged to meet at a pub and half an hour later Kevin called to offer to wait for me outside. That was considerate because I didn't want to walk in on my own. Still, everyone in there fell silent the moment they saw me.

Kevin and I sat in a quiet corner and talked all night, and I drank all night too. He told me how his friend phoned him and urged him to turn on his telly when news broke that the boys had been killed. He saw pictures of Steve, Bret and Brad Lee and asked his friend, 'What's happened to Dee?' The TV report didn't mention me.

He knew Steve because they both drank at the Old Oscott working men's club so I didn't need to try to explain what he was really like. It always sounded so unbelievable to most people. Steve had classed Kevin as one of his best friends but Kevin, like the majority of people he drank with, thought Steve was an utter idiot: he drank with Steve to keep the peace.

Kevin also knew Bret and Brad Lee because when I was working Steve took them to the club. While Steve spent hours getting pissed, Kevin taught them how to play snooker. He thought Steve was a bit jealous about that. It was comforting hearing Kevin recall how Bret and Brad Lee were so polite and funny. I loved it when people talked about them like that.

Kevin asked how I was coping and at last I could admit I wasn't. He seemed patient, understanding and interested in what I had to say. I was so comfortable pouring out my innermost feelings and fears to him. He was calm, gentle, wise and a good listener – everything Steve was not.

We weren't finished talking by the time the club closed so we went back to Kevin's house in nearby Kingstanding to carry on. But I wasn't in control of my drinking then so when I woke the next day, fully clothed and alone in Kevin's bed, I was mortified.

Kevin had slept downstairs on the couch but woke me by knocking on the door and bringing in a cup of coffee.

'I'm really sorry I got so drunk,' I said. 'I can't remember a thing about getting here.'

Kevin said, 'You were all right, you've got a reason to get drunk. No one thinks less of you.'

I thought Kevin wouldn't want to see me again after I'd been so plastered but he did. I'd found someone I could really talk to.

Kevin was nice to me every time we met. I had my guard up, but he seemed to get everything about me from the off. He would hold my hand as I cried, or gently rub my shoulder. Such small signs of niceness felt good after such a traumatic time.

The day he invited me to his immaculate house for lunch, things changed. When I got there and saw the table set with flowers, candles and wine, I thought, 'Uh oh.'

As we ate, Kevin played a Feargal Sharkey song I'd never heard before. He said the lyrics said it all. it was about offering to love another man's woman if he ever broke her heart or treated her unkindly.

Two weeks later, we had our first kiss.

I didn't go home to Mum's house much after that. Whenever I was with Kevin, I told my family I was with Tanya. In fact, Tanya – my friend from the oldest profession – had been with me at the worst moment of my life and came to the boys' funerals, but we drifted apart after that. It must have been hard for a young woman in her twenties to try to understand everything I'd gone through, to try to empathise and advise. So I didn't want to offload on to her and preferred my own company.

People said it was too soon to get together with Kevin. Our relationship was condemned by all who knew us. Even Kevin and I knew it was wrong but it felt right.

There is no road map, no rule book about how long you should wait to find love after a bereavement or horrific time. It happened quickly for me and too quickly for everyone else.

We knew people were whispering that maybe Kevin and I had got together when the boys were still alive and that's why Steve killed them. But that is not true. Anyone who even vaguely knew Steve knows it would have been impossible for me to even have a short conversation with another man or Steve would have smashed every bone in his body – and mine.

We got together after Steve did what he did. I know that, and Kevin knows that. My conscience is clear on that one. But we were both stunned when Kevin received a poison pen letter from Steve, sent from his remand prison. He addressed it to the Old Oscott working men's club. One of the committee members asked Kevin to sit down, poured him a drink and then handed him the letter.

It warned Kevin to stay away from me because I wasn't to be trusted and was evil. It said I had arranged for Albanian gangsters to kill our beautiful boys and that Bret and Brad Lee had been his world.

The letter made me fume. Even the very fact that he was free to write one infuriated me. But I wasn't surprised that even when he was locked up he was still trying to stir up trouble. He just wouldn't give up; his malice knew no bounds.

Fortunately, Kevin knew Steve and now he knew me. The letter shook us but didn't damage our relationship at all. I know it sounds like something out of a slushy romance novel, but Kevin and I really did feel like we were meant to be.

And it nearly never happened. Kevin was dating another woman around the time of the boys' deaths but when he started spending time with me he called it off and told her, even before he told me, that he had feelings for me and wanted to spend time with me.

At 38, Kevin was 12 years older than me. He had been married for 10 years before but his wife left in November 2001 and moved to Scotland when their marriage broke down. He was bringing up his three kids with the help of his mum, who looked after them when he was out working as a landscape gardener. Leanne was 14, Scott was 12 and Sophie was 11 when we first met.

It was weird when I was first introduced to Kevin's children. I had to ask myself, 'Am I ready for this? Can I look after and love someone else's kids when I miss my own so much?'

But I could, and I did.

Kevin's introduction to my family didn't result in a series of hearty backslaps and warm handshakes. They'd not suspected a thing and just thought I'd been spending time with Tanya. So one night, at the old club where they still drank, I brought Kevin in and said, 'Mum, Dave – meet Tanya.'

'This is all a bit soon, don't you think?' was Dave's response.

'Imagine what people will say, Dee,' said Mum.

But I didn't care. I had been staring into an abyss when Kevin Griffiths came along. If I hadn't met him, hadn't felt such a strong connection to him, I definitely would have killed myself. He gave me a new reason to live.

Kevin and I met each other's family only a few weeks after becoming a couple, which sounds way too fast, but it was necessary: I was pregnant.

Chapter 19
Mother And Son Again

Owen William Griffiths was born on 13 November 2002. He was nine weeks premature and tiny at only 3lb 14oz. I had a son again. And delicate as he was, he was perfect and heart-achingly beautiful.

Kevin was thrilled to bits. And having my new little bundle of life reignited my own. I felt engulfed in love as soon as I saw him, the same overwhelming sense of adoration I'd had when Bret and Brad Lee were born. But I was so different now. I was not the scared, naive, dominated teenager I had been the last time I was on this same maternity ward. I had been burned by trauma and hardened by life but now I had a small and helpless angel of new hope.

Everything about Owen's arrival, from my pregnancy to his birth and his early weeks in the world, was difficult.

Yes, I got pregnant too soon. Kevin and I knew that. But once the test said positive so were we. It was a pity, yet understandable, that no one around us felt the same.

Kevin told my mum I was pregnant. 'She'd better not be,' was the response.

I told Dave. 'I hope you know what you're doing,' he said.

Amanda sucked air through her teeth when I broke the news to her. 'The defence will use your pregnancy as a motive,' she said. 'Steve could stand in the witness box and say you'd been with Kevin all along and that's why he did it.'

I was desperate to see Steve go down, so I hated the thought I was dealing him what he thought was a trump card, even if it meant more months of waiting for the trial. As luck would have it, the prosecution asked to move the case from November 2002 to March 2003 as they needed more time for their investigations. That was a huge relief for me because I was due on 19 January.

It was hard to disguise my condition because it was such a tough pregnancy. I was sick every day and felt so exhausted that every waking hour felt like walking through treacle. The stress of Steve's impending trial bore heavily and really wore me out. It meant I could never relax, could rarely sleep or even sit still for long.

Throughout my pregnancy, I fretted constantly about what people would say when they knew I was expecting again so soon. And if they thought having another baby would mean I'd forget about Bret and Brad Lee, they were outrageously far off the mark. I tortured myself about the very fact I was pregnant – had I got myself into another inescapable situation? And what if I couldn't love my new baby as much as Bret and Brad Lee?

Kevin calmed me down. Whenever we were alone we loved placing our hands on my baby bump, feeling the gentle movements that proved there really was a little being in there.

We were excited about the thought of having a child together, thrilled that our unborn baby was already cementing us as a new family but we couldn't share that happiness with anyone else.

I was around six months gone when I was invited to the unveiling of a memorial bench for Bret and Brad Lee at Grove Vale Primary School. It was a lovely gesture and so moving to think the bench will be there forever and that future generations will read its plaque and learn about my boys.

In front of the bench they planted bulbs in the shape of intertwined letter Bs. And they also showed me their plans for an adventure playground dedicated to Bret and Brad Lee because the headteacher, Mr Leivers, wanted pupils to remember the happy times they'd had with my sons. I posed for pictures with the bench for the local newspaper and if you look really carefully you can see my bump.

Eleven weeks before my baby's due date, I felt the sharp, breath-stopping pains of labour and a friend called Neil drove me and Kevin to hospital, as Kevin can't drive a manual car which is what we had at the time. After steroid injections into my leg and an overnight stay, doctors said I was free to go home as long as I rested.

Two weeks later, the pains returned. This time doctors said, 'It's gone too far this time. There's nothing we can do to stop the baby coming today.'

I know a lot of women give midwives hell during the excruciating pain of giving birth but I fear I was the worst they'd ever had. I was a right bitch – I swore at them the whole way through and the agony seemed to give me the excuse to scream out years of pent-up rage. Flashbacks of Bret and Brad Lee traumatised me at this already distressing time. Scenes of the recurring nightmare played whenever I squeezed my eyes shut. I yelled foul words I'd never uttered before.

The midwives asked if I was having my first baby, and I think Kevin quietly told them my first two babies were now dead. He was so overwhelmed when he saw Owen he cried – and I apologised to the midwives. They were so gracious and nice to try to understand. Some suggested I went to another hospital for Owen's birth, but I was so happy when I first saw Bret and Brad Lee that I specifically wanted to be at Sandwell Hospital. When I'd given birth to them in this very delivery suite, those first minutes of holding my babies made the labour and birthing pain disappear. But I could not hold Owen – he was so fragile he had to be rushed straight into intensive care. I knew there was talk among the doctors that perhaps my baby wouldn't make it, but I shut that out: it was unthinkable.

I rarely left Owen's incubator. I sat there, gazing at him and with my hand pressed up against the glass, desperate for my new son to grow strong enough to be free of the tubes that fed him and kept him alive so I could cuddle him. I ached to feel his head between the crook of my neck and my cheek – the area of the body women never really use until they become mothers and nestle a baby there. Owen had too many wires and monitors to easily allow that. Stroking his hand was as much contact as I could safely have.

Owen was a gorgeous baby. He had a shock of black hair and, because he was so premature, his titchy little body was also quite hairy so we called him our little monkey. Kevin chose his name – he is an ardent Liverpool fan so our son is named after Michael Owen.

The neonatal intensive care unit is well secured with its cameras over the combination lock buzzer door. The rules of etiquette were explained to all parents on the ward. We should never pick up another mother's baby or even peer into another incubator. I was glad of such rigid rules because my instincts to protect Owen were ramped up to such an extent that I was ferocious: I would let no harm come to him, no one horrible near him. My paranoia extended even to my closest family.

Nicky's son Benjamin was born with Hunter syndrome and regularly came to hospital to receive medicine and therapy. He just happened to be seen in the room next door to the special care ward. One morning, when I had nipped away from the ward for a shower, Nicky popped in to see Owen.

'Oh, Dee – I have seen Owen and he is just beautiful!'

I should have been flattered but I was furious and as soon as I arrived back on the ward I had a massive go at the nurses.

'How DARE you let my sister in to see my baby!' I said.

'But we assumed it would be OK – she *is* your sister.'

'I don't care if she was my sister or not. You shouldn't have let anyone in to see my son without my consent. Anyone could say they were my sister.'

A week later, I stopped dead in my tracks when I arrived at the special care ward first thing in the morning to see Owen's incubator empty. A group of nurses were standing nearby, holding babies. Thanks to his mass of spiky hair, I spotted Owen right away.

The nurse said, 'Owen has been a very naughty boy today, Mummy.'

How could a wee scrap of a baby, who had the smallest size nappy fastened up around his chest, be naughty?

'He took off his nappy and pooed all over the incubator,' the nurse said. 'We had to take Owen out so we could clean it.'

I was relieved and delighted. Our baby boy clearly had a fighting spirit. I'd been scared to assume he'd be OK, frightened to imagine how I'd feel if I lost another son. But when Owen had his little dirty protest I had a feeling he would make it.

Owen was allowed home on 11 December but Christmas was strange that year. I was bereft without Bret and Brad Lee but full of love for little Owen. He was the gift I couldn't stop looking at and feeling thankful for. I was glad to be without Steve and to have Kevin instead.

And Kevin did everything he could to make Christmas lovely for his children and me. I admired him so much and appreciated every cup of tea he made, every gift he wrapped. It was the saddest yet warmest Christmas I'd ever had.

Kevin had put up with so much from me. I was horrible to him – I had temper tantrums that flared up out of nowhere and would throw his genuine care and concern back in his face.

'How do you know how I feel? How can you care?'

Even when my voice rose to a scream Kevin stayed calm – 'Dee, I'm trying my best to understand, but you won't let me in to help you.'

No one understood how I was dealing with grief, a new relationship and a newborn son all at the same time. Those major life events were jammed into 10 months and brought with them a potent mix of hormones. I got through it because I was numb.

But then, one snowy night, everything came crashing down. I picked an argument with Kevin over nothing, dropped his mobile phone into his drink and then threw the drink over him. As soon as I did it I felt so ashamed that I ran outside and sat, sobbing, in the snow. Kevin tried everything he could to coax me in but I was vile to him, saying, 'Just leave me alone, I want to be dead!'

And I could not move. I stayed there for five hours, shivering and sobbing. In the end Kevin called my sister Angie and she carried me back to the house. I stayed in bed for four days after that. I couldn't get warm and I couldn't get out of bed, even though I knew I'd left Kevin to look after baby Owen on his own.

That's when I experienced the abject fear, hopelessness, exhaustion and deep woe of a full nervous breakdown.

Chapter 20
The Trial Begins

Steve's trial began at Birmingham Crown Court on Wednesday, 10 March 2003.

I had an angry need to be there to hear every minute of testimony, to make Steve look me in the eye and to listen to every lie that spouted from his mouth so I could contest it. But Kevin and Amanda didn't want me in court every day – they said I wouldn't cope with what I would no doubt hear. And they were probably right. The rage I felt whenever Steve loomed into my thoughts was so extreme it made me shake.

To protect the integrity of the trial, Amanda had to keep many details she'd gleaned about Steve's defence case from me despite the endless hours we spent talking. She promised to attend court throughout and phone me during each break in proceedings. Her first call, on the morning when I was due to give evidence, floored me.

'Denise, the prosecution barrister has just made his opening statements. He said Steve was never in the SAS. He wasn't trained to kill. He only served 138 days in the regular Army 25 years ago and was kicked out for fighting.'

I was stunned. If Gemma, Konrad, Stacey and I had known that, we would never have been so scared. And yet I *should* have known. The cowardly act of killing two little boys wasn't the action of someone in the elite forces. There was nothing fearless, brave, special or highly trained about a man who frequently beat up his wife. Yet Steve had told that SAS lie from our first date and used it to intimidate me, his kids, friends, neighbours – everyone. It was his excuse for his violent rages. I had begged him not to go on so-called missions because I worried for his safety, and that manipulative pig used my misplaced concern as the reason to force me out to work and to rob me of time with my sons. Pathetic, disgusting liar!

I knew it didn't really matter what I wore to court – it only mattered what I said. But I wanted to make a good impression because I was representing Bret and Brad Lee. Amanda not only advised me what to wear, she also let me go through her wardrobe of sophisticated clothes and borrow a long black skirt and classy-looking beige jacket. Wearing something that Steve had chosen was out of the question. Imagine how smug he would have been to see me in something he'd paid for.

Dressing up as smartly as I could was also a way of building my confidence and bolstering my strength so I could get through my appearance at the trial – like armour, in a way. I needed that extra layer of support because it was so hard to turn up at that court. I didn't want to be under the same roof as Steve, didn't want to be near enough to breathe the same air. I knew his barrister would try to trip me up and twist my words but I wasn't too stressed about that because all I could do was tell the truth and naturally the full story would come out with no contradictions. The cause of my anxiety and heavy sense of foreboding wasn't about giving evidence, it was about seeing Steve.

Amanda met me at court and had to counsel me calm.

'He won't be able to escape and get at me in court, will he?' I asked.

'No, Denise. Absolutely no way. He will be flanked by police officers and it will be impossible for him to get to you,' she reassured me.

'Because you know he will kill me, don't you? He won't stop until he's killed me too.'

'Denise, I promise you. You will be protected and he will be guarded by police. I swear.'

Amanda held my hand until seconds before I had to take the stand. And there I was, all alone, glaring at that villainous man who had created my children and then destroyed them. Barely 15 feet away in the dock, he looked like he hadn't shaved, hadn't slept and didn't care. He wore jeans and a grey checked shirt, as if this trial for the murder of his two sons was no big deal. But he looked older, smaller. And he wore a gold cross around his neck, which was meant to convince us all he was a God-loving good man. But there was no mistaking evil, I'd have recognised him a mile off. The sight of him made me feel sick – and terrified.

Steve wouldn't look at me. Instead, he just stared down at the notes he had on the shelf of the dock and scribbled on them. He probably thought he could direct proceedings, that he could out-smart all the top-class QCs and solicitors there.

The courtroom was packed. I saw reporters scribbling furiously into notepads, the jury looking serious, my sisters in the public gallery. There was no one on the family benches for Steve.

As I took my oath on the Bible, all faces in court turned to mine but after a few minutes on the stand they blurred. The only people I was aware of were Steve and David Crigman QC, the prosecution barrister, who gently but very directly asked me questions, which allowed me to paint the picture of my truly awful life with my husband.

There was not a sound in the court when I told how Steve had first hit me when I was pregnant with Bret. How he had battered me around a hundred times since then. About the time he head-butted me and broke my nose, of his many assaults that saw me hospitalised. About the pool-ball attack, which left me crippled for almost a week.

'He would push me up against the wall and put his finger in the left side of my throat. He would say that, if he pushed any harder, he would kill me. He beat me, kicked me, put pillows over my face and tried to strangle me.'

David Crigman QC said that on the night of 6 February, after I'd thrown myself from his car, Steve circled the area looking for me. And I had a weird feeling then: if he'd found me, he'd have killed me. Bret and Brad Lee would still have had their chance at life. I wished I could have saved them such pain, such terror. Wished I could have sacrificed my own life for theirs.

I tried to explain how fear had prevented me from progressing with the scores of police complaints I'd made. Also how I'd believed Bret and Brad Lee should not be separated from their father, which was why I returned home after leaving him repeatedly to escape to refuges. I described how my tyrant of a husband forced me into prostitution, which pushed me over the edge and made me leave him for good.

'It was the children that kept me with him. He mentioned that he had good SAS friends – they would track me down. He mentioned he would never give up and he would find me if I ever took his kids off him.

'I suppose I just got fed up from being abused and battered and just found the strength from somewhere.'

It was agonisingly hard to relive every step of that meeting at McDonald's, my last beating from Steve and his 12-second call to tell me what he'd done to my precious Bret and Brad Lee.

I sobbed so much I found it hard to catch my breath long enough to speak clearly. The court had to be adjourned so I could compose myself. Steve would have loved that – he'd have celebrated the fact I was too weak to go on. But I just could not do it. After a strong cup of tea and an intense pep talk from Amanda, I went back on the witness stand with renewed determination to tell my side – the truthful side – of what Steve had done.

'He called me and said, "I've just killed the kids and I'm trying to kill myself." He said it in an evil way, an aggressive way. I was all panicking because I couldn't hear the children in the background.'

When Mr Crigman had finished questioning me and sat down, I was exhausted. Recalling the worst moments of my life in such a formal setting, knowing my words were vital to the punishment Steve would or would not receive, was one of the hardest challenges I'd ever faced. But I had no idea that I'd just been through the easy bit. Cross-examination by Steve's defence counsel, Patrick Thomas QC, was so harrowing it brought me perilously close to collapse: I felt like I was the one on trial.

Mr Thomas insisted Steve had not blackmailed me into a life of vice. And what happened next caused my stomach to spasm. A film of me with the Asian man I'd had sex with in the cabin was shown to the court. There I was, smiling a fake smile and taking his money. Minutes later, not shown on the tape, I'd given the cash in full to Steve.

I was reeling. Until that moment I'd had no idea Steve had rigged up cameras to capture me with a client. Now my most shameful act of prostitution would be reported to the nation.

Steve's plan to shred my reputation was working. I had no time to steady myself before I was hit with more accusations from his barrister.

'In fact, you were perfectly comfortable with being a prostitute – it was your chosen way of life...'

No, no way! I felt dizzy with the injustice of hearing what couldn't have been further from the truth. And it got worse. The defence counsel accused me of raiding a safe at the Fingertips brothel and then disappearing with cocaine and cash, which they said I'd spent on alloy wheels and antique guns for Steve.

Absolutely not. I had never taken drugs in my life. I had the keys to the safe at Fingertips, yes. But I had not stolen from the safe, not ever. Around that time I had left Steve and forgotten that the Fingertips keys were at home, so I bet he stole the money. I am sure that's why he didn't argue when I told him I didn't want to go back after he'd paid for sex with the girls there. And there he was, trying to turn everything around and pin his crimes on me.

The barrister outlined Steve's fantasist claims of being targeted by Albanian pimps who wanted revenge for stealing their earnings and drugs from the Fingertips safe. He said Steve was fearful his family would be targeted over the stolen money and wanted the guns put in the pool room in case of an attack. It was all ludicrous lies – the only attack his family had endured was from Steve. The only one who wanted me to be a prostitute was Steve.

And then came the defence barrister's knockout blow. I had constantly blamed myself for Bret and Brad Lee's deaths and everyone vehemently told me it was Steve's fault, not mine. But now I was being blamed by a barrister in front of the entire court.

Mr Thomas prodded his finger at me and said, 'You lied to your husband and said you were merely a receptionist at the massage parlour. You were a prostitute. You stole money for drugs. YOU are the one who had your boys killed.'

'*No!*' I said. 'My kids meant the world to me. I am not an evil person.'

No, no, no, no, *no*!

The instant my evidence was over I fled the court in tears.

Chapter 21
Poor And Elaborate Fiction

Back home that evening, I could barely let go of Owen. Even when he fell asleep I wanted to feel him on my chest, hold him as tightly as I could. I needed to be close to his purity and innocence, to let him feel all the love I had for him as well as Bret and Brad Lee. I felt so disgustingly dirty, seeing that film of myself and being in such close proximity to Steve. Cuddling Owen helped me see the hope in my life. My baby boy reminded me that being a good mum and being happy should really be quite simple – all we needed was love.

Kevin was amazing. He just seemed to know when I needed to be left alone to be quiet and had a sixth sense for when I needed to talk about light or dark things. When I felt like ranting about Steve or crying over happy memories of Bret and Brad Lee, he was a sympathetic listener. When I took myself off to be alone and buried my face in a pillow to sob, I'd lift my head an hour later to see that Kevin had left a cup of tea by my bedside. Sometimes he just held me and that was all I needed. He wrapped his arms around me every night in bed and made me feel loved for the first time in my life.

I wanted to stay cosseted at home with Owen and Kevin and to close the door to the outside world but Steve's trial was rumbling on and I had to be there.

The next day, the newspaper reports on the trial covered my time in the witness stand. I was described in the first line of a story as 'a former prostitute'. Another headline ran: 'TRAGIC MUM'S SEX VIDEO'. It felt I was being kicked when I was truly down.

The reports carried the prosecution barrister's opening speech, which I'd missed because I was outside the courtroom preparing to give evidence. The description of Steve's actions, thoughts and motivations was so accurate it was as if the barrister had been right there with me throughout my last decade.

David Crigman QC told the jury Steve had spent the four days between my leaving and the boys' deaths 'sitting at home brooding and bridling at her resistance. He demanded control'.

He went on, 'He drove to a dark and cold and a very secluded place. He was seething. One of the themes of this case is control. This defendant demanded control of this woman. But he knew he could no longer control his wife. Apart from seething, he was wallowing in self-pity. He then took what he saw as being the ultimate revenge by killing their two children.'

Mr Crigman explained to the court that they could not be certain which of my boys died first but they believed that it had been Brad Lee because Bret had injuries consistent with a struggle.

He said, 'We will never know what Steve said to Bret but we know in a 999 call after the incident he told the operator that the children wanted to die with him so that they could all go to Heaven. Bret must have watched on in horror.

'The venom against his wife was such that he wanted to teach her a lesson she would never forget. This was the most vicious way he could strike back at her because she had left him.'

Reading the outline of Steve's defence left me bitterly incredulous.

'Wilson allegedly told police two masked men murdered the boys. Wilson said the mystery pair stabbed them because his wife had stolen money from a sauna where she was working.

'He said he was followed by a black BMW to the golf course by the men, one armed with a gun.

'He said, "The gunman sat in front of my car and pointed the gun at me and the second masked man got into the back. He knocked the hell out of Bret. He put a screwdriver to my neck and asked me where the money was. He said there were drugs and documents as well. He pulled the screwdriver out and stabbed me a few times. Then I woke up and found the children dead. I stabbed myself three more times. I found out Denise was doing prostitution."'

Steve's defence was a work of poor and elaborate fiction.

Unfortunately, despite Kevin and Amanda doing their utmost to shield me from stark details, there was no hiding the terrible facts of Bret and Brad Lee's deaths once they were splashed all over the papers. I had to run to the loo to vomit when I read the reports.

'In the car Wilson carried a weapon, it was a weapon he said for innocent purposes – a Stanley knife blade pushed into a beer mat.

'He got into the back of the vehicle, he cut Brad's throat. He did it with two slashing wounds across the left side of the neck and in doing that he broke off the little tip of his weapon.

'It had rendered the weapon now useless so he took up a screwdriver and stabbed the child in one of the open wounds to ensure the child was killed.'

I could scarcely believe I was reading about my own boys, my own life. I hated thinking of their perfect, soft skin being slashed and their precious lives seeping away. I wished I could stop imagining their terror at seeing their dad do what he did and their dashed hopes that Mummy would save them. It made me weep and crumple with sorrow and regret. Attending court again was the last thing I wanted to do but I had to.

When Konrad took the stand, I had no idea how his evidence would go. Would he bravely tell the truth and testify against his own father? Or would he lie and prove the truth of the old adage 'blood is thicker than water'?

Konrad began by telling the jury how he had seen his father's violence towards me several times. Then he recounted the evening of Bret and Brad Lee's attacks.

Konrad said, 'Dad rang and said, "Sorry, mate, for killing your brothers." He told me he had stabbed Bret in the throat with a screwdriver and killed Brad as well.

'He said that he had punched Dee but she got away from the car. He said he couldn't handle it any longer and that he was going to die with the lads and that they were all going to go together.'

During two phone calls from his dad, Konrad said Steve 'laughed at one point and never told me where he was'.

Konrad asked him if he'd really done it, Steve said, 'I know when somebody is dead, mate, because they haven't been breathing for 15 minutes.'

It seems that when Steve was in prison on remand he cooked up his tale about gangsters and became a prolific letter writer. Konrad told the court Steve had written to him claiming Albanian assassins had targeted him and the boys.

As an extract from the letter was read out to the court, Steve, who was wearing rosary beads alongside his crucifix, broke down in tears. In his letter he said he would 'take the blame for this' and would 'never hurt Bret and Brad'.

Konrad's testimony against his dad was damning, so when the defence barrister stood to begin his cross-examination I held my breath.

But Konrad buried Steve even deeper.

Patrick Thomas QC asked Konrad if he hated his father and he replied, 'Yes.'

When Mr Thomas claimed Steve had been threatened by gangsters, he asked Konrad if his dad had been living in fear.

'No,' said Konrad. 'Everyone else was living in fear of him.'

Stacey gave evidence against Steve too and told how she had seen him being violent towards me.

I was moved by Konrad and Stacey's testimony. I was so sad that they had also endured so much suffering at their own dad's hands yet proud of them for telling the truth. How I wished all of our truths could have been different.

Tapes of Steve's 999 calls were played out in court later that day. I cried listening to the heavy, stressed breathing I'd also heard that terrible evening. Hearing Steve steadfastly withhold his whereabouts, knowing Bret and Brad Lee were bleeding to death, made my knuckles turn white with rage. Emergency operators pleaded with Steve to tell them where he was and he lied by saying he was in Bewdley, then the Wyre Forest in Worcestershire. His first of three calls was made at 8.48pm and in total they lasted 90 minutes – all the while Bret and Brad Lee lay dead beside him.

The tapes were harrowingly clear. Steve said, 'I have killed the kids and I'm going to kill myself now. My wife, Denise Wilson, she always said that the kids were little bastards and that she wishes she never had them. She has got what she wants now. She can have her own way now. She's a prostitute. There's a video on the top of the bed showing her having sex with another man.

'She has left, that is why I have done it. We were always in her way. She has wrecked our lives. I love them that much I want to die with them. I love my kids to death. I have stabbed my kids and I will stab myself and we will all go together.

'I stabbed my son in the neck with a screwdriver and I have done myself in the neck with the screwdriver. I couldn't find my heart. Why can't I fucking die?'

In the final call Steve said, 'They are dead in the car. I am loving them, I have got my arms around them.

'I am getting weak now, I have stabbed myself in the throat six times and all down my arms.

'She has got what she wants now. I have told her that the children are dead, she said, "I have a lovely life now."

'My kids are with me, they are lying side by side of me; they are dead.'

Every person in the courtroom who heard those tapes looked distressed – except Steve. He stared straight ahead and sat expressionless throughout.

There was more traumatic evidence to come. The next witness was WPC Karen Huxley from West Bromwich police station, one of the first officers on the scene. It wasn't her fault because she was only doing her job, but listening to her description of finding Bret and Brad Lee dead in Steve's car was the worst moment in my life since the boys' deaths.

She said she had searched for more than an hour to find Steve and the boys. When she came across their car, it had no lights on and the doors were closed.

Karen said, 'The man in the vehicle was sitting on the left-hand side behind the driver's seat.

'He had a mobile phone to his ear and his other hand was on the chest of the smallest child. Next to the male was a child lying on his back with his head and shoulders on the seat. His head was back and his eyes were open. The child had a cut underneath his throat, which was gaping open. It was cut from one side to the other.'

Karen said she checked to see if Brad Lee was still breathing but found that he wasn't. Then she checked on Steve.

'The man sitting next to this child had a red-handled screwdriver sticking out of his chest, about seven to eight inches. Sitting farthest away from him was another child, who was slightly bigger.

'He was lying face down, his body and his shoulders were on the seat and he was in the kneeling position.'

Karen said officers decided to get Bret and Brad Lee out of the car and attempt resuscitation, as ambulance crews did not arrive until 30 minutes after the boys were found.

She said Steve was taken out of the car, handcuffed and sat in the police car, where officers watched him.

Under cross-examination Karen denied claims by Steve's defence barrister, Mr Thomas, that Steve had been 'manhandled by officers'.

Mr Thomas asked, 'By being forceful you thought you will kill him?'

She replied, 'No.'

How disgusting of Steve, who always tried to play the victim, that after savagely murdering his two children he whinged about alleged rough handling by the police. How ridiculous to have claimed that an officer tried to kill him.

I just wish they had.

Chapter 22
Lies, Lies, Lies

I knew Steve was evil. I knew his malevolence was limitless. But even I was shocked to hear how speedily his warped mind worked to invent lies minutes after he had slashed his two sons to death.

A nurse called Sheila Wilkinson was the next witness on the stand. I flinched when I heard that she was the first to treat Steve when he arrived at Sandwell Hospital – the place of Bret, Brad Lee and now Owen's birth. Her description of Steve's calm demeanour was chilling.

Sheila said, 'He was in pain and kept talking, it was a continuous monologue. He was calm and cool throughout. Wilson told me his wife was a prostitute and he'd recently recovered from a sexually transmitted disease that she had given him. He said the children put a video on the VCR with his wife and an Asian man having sex. Wilson said the children were in Heaven. He kept saying, "The boys said we want to be in Heaven, Daddy."'

Sheila told the jury she had held Steve's hand because he was frightened after being admitted to the hospital's emergency unit with a screwdriver embedded up to the handle in his chest. That made me fume: Steve, a double child killer, was in hospital having his hand held by a kindly nurse because he was in a tiny bit of pain. But who had held my sons' hands as they lay dying?

Sheila continued, 'He said he had done something silly and asked to hold my hand because he was in pain. He talked about his marital life regarding his wife and children. He said he was frightened. He just kept on that the children were safe now. He told me his wife was a prostitute. He carried on about his first wife, who died of cancer.'

Even in such horrific circumstances, Steve's first thoughts were of Trish.

His attempts at suicide were glaringly half-hearted because, according to a surgeon who treated him, he didn't even need a single stitch.

Dr David Gourevich told the jury that all Steve's wounds were superficial, only penetrating the skin and fat underneath. He said, 'None of the injuries caused any medical concern. The screwdriver had missed all the vital organs and there was no significant blood loss. I did nothing to the wound in his chest but clean it.'

I had suspected as much. I knew Steve wouldn't want to kill himself because he wanted to see my pain at what he had done.

CCTV footage recording Steve's journey to the golf course was shown to the court. I could be clearly seen sitting in the car with the boys opposite the tram station in West Bromwich.

It was like watching a scene from a horror film that seemed too far-fetched to be my real life. I wanted to pause the tape, change the plot, get the kids out of the car and give the story a happy ending.

The court was then shown infra-red images from a police helicopter video, which showed a light beaming on to the car at the golf course. It was so strange to see a still from my recurring nightmare on film. Again it reinforced to me that, sadly, it really did happen.

A Home Office pathologist called Dr Peter Acland then told of my boys' devastating injuries. He said, 'It looks as if the attacker was deliberately aiming for the vital structures of the neck. Damage to the carotid artery in the neck is normally a catastrophic event.'

Carotid arteries, I knew it.

When asked about Bret's injuries, Dr Acland said, 'These are all restraint-type injuries from holding a child still. There's obviously been some physical struggle and probably some blows from a short distance or banging against a structure.

'There was obviously physical violence and struggles. Both boys would have died within five or six minutes.'

I knew I could not cope any more. The precise details of my boys' suffering being described in such a cold, scientific way was necessary, I understood that. But I didn't just hear the factual statements in that laboratory report – I heard Bret and Brad Lee's infectious laughs, their sweet voices saying, 'We love you,

Mummy, we do.' And I heard their screams as they saw the man who was meant to love and protect them more than anyone in the world turn on them so brutally.

To me, that evidence was far more than the conclusion of a study of measurements taken from two corpses on a mortuary slab. It was an all-too-clear description of my boys' pain and I felt every thrust of the knife, every stab of the screwdriver. I knew that each blow robbed the warmth of their bodies and spirit.

Being in the same room as the monster who did that made me feel faint and yet Steve showed not a flicker of grief, shame or sadness for his sons. He just stared straight ahead at the judge, completely devoid of emotion, the entire time.

Even when presented with photos of Bret and Brad Lee's fatal injuries, which made the jurors flinch and blanch, he just stuck yellow sticky notes on them as if he was some hot-shot lawyer and clever enough to represent himself. He never once looked at me, and I never once looked away from him. My eyes bored undiluted, burning hatred into him. I was so churned up inside I knew I was edging close to another nervous breakdown.

After my meltdown in the snow, my GP had given me anti-depressants, which I took for a few months before weaning myself off them. They made me feel I was living in cuckoo land and I couldn't live in a false world like that, but being in court that day pushed me to the brink of emotional collapse again. So the next day I decided to stay home with Owen. And I was so glad to be there. Steve had snatched away my eldest two sons and I would not let him steal any more of my precious moments with my youngest.

Then I got a call from Amanda.

'Denise, you've been recalled to court. You really need to come straight away.'

'I can't. I've got no one to babysit Owen.'

'I'll look after him. You can't walk into court with him because the press will see you and they'll put two and two together to get five.'

Within minutes, she arrived in a car to pick me up and we strapped Owen into a car seat. When we arrived at court, Amanda waited in the car for 15 minutes after I got out. Once the flurry of photographers' flashbulbs had ended and I was in court, she carried Owen straight into a family room annexe. I would not have my baby son in the courtroom; I would not allow Steve's hate-filled eyes even to glance at him.

As I entered court I met Michael, my old boss from the chip shop, who was leaving.

'Michael, what are you doing here?'

'Denise, I am so sorry. I can't imagine what you're going through. I was called as a witness. I told the court about how Steve smashed up my car, and me.'

I had been so ashamed of Steve battering my boss. And now I was so grateful to Michael for telling the jury all about it.

I was called back to the stand to answer a question about stabbing Steve with the scissors in April 2000. Straight away I admitted it and explained that I'd done it as a knee-jerk reaction to him kicking my back with ferocious force.

I said, 'When you have been abused so much you retaliate. I just flipped and stabbed him in the arm. Steve didn't go to hospital. Instead he sat on the edge of the bath and stitched the wound himself with black cotton – he said he was like Rambo.'

Steve's barrister went on to accuse me of putting glass and rat poison into Steve's tea.

'No, definitely not,' I said. 'But I wish I'd thought of that.'

Next it was Steve's turn to give his evidence. I knew, even before he opened his mouth, that the court would hear nothing but falsehoods and fabrication. And I was right.

Tapes of Steve's first police interviews were played before he took the stand. The court heard him say he had no explanation for Bret and Brad Lee's deaths – a story he would drastically change.

He said, 'I parked the car there and I was thinking, I will phone tomorrow when Denise is calmed down. Then the boys started saying they didn't want to see her again, that she was horrible, and they were talking about the videotape.

'I was sitting there and all me head was going funny and, you know, I got in the back and sat with the boys and then I was loving them.

'I was asking them why and they were saying, "Her's dirty and horrible and she might hurt us," and they just wanted to stay with me.

'I looked down and I had my hands on the babies and blood everywhere, and I was trying to see if they were still alive.

'I couldn't find their pulse. I was sure they were dead. I watched me wife die and everything. I held her in my arms when she died.

'I wanted to go with them – I wanted to be with my babies. I don't know what happened, I have got no explanation.'

He told officers that Bret and Brad Lee were 'petrified' of me because I was always 'in a mood and threw tea in their eyes and threatened to take them to a naughty home'.

He said his relationship with the boys had been 'fantastic'.

Lies, lies, lies.

Steve also insisted that I had invented his assault on me that day in the car outside McDonald's.

He said I'd attacked him and had lashed out with my fists. Pushing the boundaries of belief, he even suggested I'd caused my black eye by 'thumping' myself and insisted he had acted in self-defence.

If the situation hadn't been so grotesque, if my heart hadn't been so bleak, I'd have found his interviews laughable.

The evidence he gave from the dock was even more ludicrous. He told the jury that he was the victim of years of abuse from me. He relished recalling how I'd stabbed his arm 'right to the bone', but said he had stitched his wound himself instead of going to hospital because he 'did not want to get my wife in trouble'. As if Steve was caring and considerate that way.

Steve was adamant he hadn't forced me into prostitution, claiming I'd 'promised faithfully' that I'd only done reception and managerial work. Then, as if he was quoting straight from a badly written crime thriller, he said I was accused by Albanian pimps of stealing cash and cocaine from the Fingertips safe. Apparently, I'd told them he was responsible.

Steve said he'd had a phone call from the brothel owner after I'd disappeared about the time of the theft. 'He was saying he would have me dealt with and that no one messes him around. He said I would end up pushing up daisies.'

He claimed he became more alarmed when the brothel owner's girlfriend called him and said, 'Do you think your children are safe at school?' And he went on to say I'd paid for a set of antique and replica weapons, including guns, which were stored in the pool room at the back of the home to 'give us protection' in the event of a visit from the pimps.

He told a far-fetched tale of how, on the evening of my boys' attacks, three Albanians had tracked him down and forced him to drive to Hill Top Golf Course. He even imitated the accent of one of the supposed gang, who had apparently told him, 'We meet at last,' and claimed he overheard the Albanian words for 'child' and 'knife'.

Then he said he had watched in horror with a screwdriver held to his throat as first Brad Lee and then Bret were slaughtered. He said, 'Bret was screaming, "Help me, Daddy!" I felt so ashamed of myself and guilty that I could not save them. I could not save my babies.'

Steve cried crocodile tears for 20 minutes as he answered his barrister's questions.

But then it was the prosecution barrister's turn to ask questions. And David Crigman QC sliced Steve up.

During his cross-examination, Mr Crigman QC branded Steve 'an inveterate and accomplished liar, who has lied and lied and lied'. I wanted to stand up and cheer when he said that. He trampled all over Steve's insistence that I was a tyrant who had physically abused him throughout our nine-year marriage, pointing out that I weighed just seven stone, while he weighed between 14 and 18 stone yet the jury were supposed to believe I was the one who 'called the shots and was violent'.

Mr Crigman then tore apart Steve's wild fantasy of Albanian gangsters. He pointed out the huge flaws in his attempt to set up a false defence in claiming he was unable to save Bret and Brad Lee because he had fallen unconscious after the masked men stabbed him through the neck.

Mr Crigman said, 'An expert surgeon had testified that your neck wound was superficial and did not even require a stitch.'

He accused Steve of fabricating the story and said, 'What you were telling the police is the actual ingredients up to the point where you killed the children. When you came to the killings you used "'It is me head, I have been attacked"'. Isn't that the truth?'

Steve replied, 'No.'

'You cannot tell the truth, Mr Wilson, can you?' said Mr Crigman.

Steve replied, 'I am telling the truth.'

Mr Crigman added, 'If there was any syllable of truth in that account you would have fought them to the death, wouldn't you?'

Steve replied, 'It was the first time in my life that there was nothing I could do. That is why I feel so terrible.'

But Mr Crigman jumped on each one of Steve's answers. 'If Albanian gangsters chased you in a car, where were their tyre marks? There is only one set – *yours*.' He went on to repeatedly ask Steve why he wasn't in tears during the 999 call he made.

Seven times Mr Crigman demanded an answer, saying, 'There you are coming around from a vicious attack, with your children mortally wounded. It was a terrifying spectacle with you in the back of the car with assassins. You telephoned 999 – tell us, was it the tone of a terrified man? It was not the tone of a man who has seen his boys butchered by assassins.'

Steve said, 'I was in a state of shock.'

Mr Crigman continued, 'I will keep asking – where were your tears?'

Finally, Steve admitted, 'There were not any. I had already cried – I had to deal with it and carry on.'

But Mr Crigman continued, 'The only person you cry for is yourself.'

When Mr Crigman told Steve he was in fact the murderer, Steve replied, 'I never, ever did anything like that, sir. I never, ever, ever hurt my children.

'The killers are still out there. I have spent the last 12 months in prison – I want the killers brought to justice. I'm on a wing full of murderers, rapists and child molesters and I am not like them.'

Mr Crigman said, 'The truth is, Mr Wilson, you sped up to the golf course, lights blazing, in a fury because of Denise.'

As his evidence drew to a close, Steve continued to insist that I was behind the murders and then said something about me that made me want to jump over the benches to kill him. That would have been justice, I could have done it without batting an eyelid. Nothing would have given me more pleasure.

Amanda and my younger sister Sarah held both my hands to comfort as well as restrain me. For in his last-ditch attempt to shred my soul, Steve told the court I had sexually molested my children.

Chapter 23
The Verdict

The closing speeches of the case were made on the eleventh day of the trial. Steve listened intently to the prosecution barrister David Crigman QC, all the while clutching his crucifix and shaking his head in denial.

'This defendant knows the details of how each child was murdered, which he could only know if he was the killer,' said Mr Crigman.

'His objective during this case is to manipulate, control, deceive and lie his way out of the acts of murder that he committed.'

Mr Crigman told the jury the phone calls Steve made to me, Konrad and the 999 operators were 'powerful evidence' that proved he was the killer. 'The 999 calls in their own right are conclusive proof of his guilt of murder.

'When he got into that car he was in control of those lives and in his self-obsessive way he took them.'

Mr Crigman dismissed Steve's defence that Albanian gangsters killed his children in revenge for my stealing cash and cocaine from a massage parlour as 'preposterous'. And he asked, if that was the case, why didn't Steve fight to help his sons?

'There is scarcely a father alive who would sit motionless and watch his boys be slaughtered. Wilson didn't lift a finger to help either of them. Instead, he got his phone and bemoaned his fate with his self-pity and self-justification. What happened in the back of that car was his revenge on his wife as a woman for walking out of his control.'

Mr Crigman rejected Steve's defence as a charade and branded him a 'killer' and a 'manipulative and deceiving liar'. He said by telling a 'pack of lies' Steve was hoping the judge would sentence him for manslaughter.

Steve's defence barrister, Patrick Thomas QC, told the jury they should only consider the evidence and not convict the accused on whether they liked or disliked him. He said there was no 'conclusive proof' that the knife found in Steve's car was the weapon that killed Brad.

'The fact is that the weapon that caused these injuries has disappeared,' said Mr Thomas. 'This case is consistent with somebody injuring Brad and taking the weapon away with them.'

Mr Thomas also said Steve had stated during police interviews that a black and yellow screwdriver was the weapon used by the masked Albanian pimps to stab my two boys and not the red-handled screwdriver that had been found by paramedics embedded in his chest.

'There is no evidence that the same screwdriver that killed the boys was the one used on Steven Wilson. There is another potential weapon missing,' he said.

Mr Thomas went on to claim that Steve had lied to police in the 999 calls and to his lawyers because 'he was ashamed he couldn't do anything to protect his boys'.

He added, 'A man may be a liar but that doesn't necessarily make him a murderer.'

I felt sure the jury would believe the prosecution case, until I heard the judge summing up. Mr Justice Hughes said jurors had to decide whether Steve had deliberately killed Bret and Brad Lee or if, as he claimed, they were killed by assassins.

'This case is about the murder of two little boys and the question that really matters is whether you are sure it is the defendant that killed them or whether it might have been somebody else who did kill them.

'He can be convicted of murder only if you are sure that he killed the boys. It is for the Crown to prove that he is guilty. It is also for the Crown to prove that a rule of law called provocation doesn't apply in this case. If it applies and the prosecution cannot prove that it doesn't apply, what it does, provocation, is to reduce the crime of murder to the lesser crime of manslaughter.'

I could not comprehend that there was any way any juror could possibly play down Steve's crimes by finding him guilty only of manslaughter. He planned the deaths of his own sons, he knew exactly what he was doing and he tried his utmost to falsely point the finger at me and masked Albanian pimps. He set out to kill my Bret and Brad Lee. The jury had to believe that. But what if they didn't? It was a thought so horrible that, as the court was dismissed to let the jury consider their verdict, I threw up in the courtroom loos.

Amanda, as always, was with me in the bathroom.

'Please, Amanda, you have to take his passport off him, because if he gets off with this, if he ever gets out, I will have to leave the country. What if he tries to kill my new family?' I said.

'Dee, you need to calm down.'

After so many long days of evidence, we assumed the six men and six women of the jury would take days to reach their conclusion but, less than an hour after they were dismissed, the jury reported that they had finished their deliberations and returned to the court to deliver their verdict.

No edge-of-the-seat courtroom drama could ever come close to fully capturing the tension a victim's family member feels during those moments, the frantic palpitations as everyone in the court jostles to sit down. The tight squeezing of hands so hot and sweaty they burn, the screaming terror inside your head and the imagined but urgent begging of 'please, please, *please*' for the right outcome. Holding your breath while the court falls to a hush as the jury foreman stands to deliver the verdict.

'Guilty.'

My body flopped, my arms flew around Amanda and my tears would not stop. In a unanimous decision reached in 55 minutes, Steve was found guilty of double murder and causing me actual bodily harm on that tragic night.

Judge Mr Justice Anthony Hughes told Steve, 'You took those boys' lives to revenge yourself on your wife. They were seven and eight and the manner in which you killed them was brutal. It was a dreadful and wicked thing to do.'

Steve, still wearing a crucifix and rosary beads around his neck, interrupted the judge to shout from the dock, 'I didn't kill my boys!'

But the judge continued, 'Nobody who heard you give evidence could believe more than an occasional word. There must be no mistake. Your hands took these boys' lives and the responsibility is yours.'

The judge ordered Steve's Daihatsu to be crushed. And that was the only trace of genuine emotion Steve showed throughout the trial. He looked like his world had collapsed then.

As the courtroom emptied, the victims' families were invited into another room. I was last in and remained at the back, where I saw all Steve's family saying thank you and shaking the hands of the prosecution team.

'He was a nasty man – he got what he deserved,' they were saying. '*Yess!* We never have to see him again.'

I was more grateful than all of them to see Steve go down and firmly shook hands with the lawyers but, as the rest stood around with victorious smiles, I left. Because what was there to celebrate? My life remained in tatters. Bret and Brad Lee were gone and the verdict wouldn't bring my kids back. I had won nothing but lost everything. Though immensely relieved at the verdict, I was not elated, not happy.

That evening I hugged Owen close as I watched the evening TV news reports of the trial. Detective Inspector Mick Moore said of Steve, 'He's an evil, violent man, who dwells in the depths of inhumanity.'

Detective Moore went on to describe Steve as cunning and said he was the first person he had come across in more than 29 years of police service for whom no one had a good word to say in his favour.

In the *Daily Mirror* the next day, a source close to the investigation said, 'Denise paid the ultimate price in losing her two children. Undoubtedly she has been further degraded by what evidence had to be brought out in this trial. He is without doubt the most loathsome individual I have ever encountered.

'Most people, whatever their crimes, have some redeeming feature. Wilson, uniquely in my experience, has none.'

Stacey was seen punching the air with both hands as she emerged from the court buildings. And Steve's parents gave a statement they said echoed the family's sentiments: 'We are disgusted, appalled and ashamed of Steven committing this cowardly attack against two small boys, but we are not surprised. He is an evil, lying, controlling, manipulative and devious bully, who is also power and money-mad. Everyone has been his victim over the years. We have been in fear for our lives from the threats of violence.'

They added that they had never seen Brad and Bret after Steve cut off all contact with them when Stacey and Konrad were only four and five.

'We are mourning the deaths of Brad and Bret with deep emotion even though we never met the boys. We did not even know how they looked until the newspapers printed their photos. We all hope he will be locked away for the remainder of his life. Then everyone can at last feel safe from his tyranny.'

Sometimes I regret not speaking to Steve's parents more. There is so much about him that I do not know and they could fill in the blanks. I feel the same about Trish's family. I assumed the people with Stacey throughout the trial were relatives from her mum's side because I didn't recognise them but I was so distrustful, so raw, that I just couldn't spend time with anyone who was related to Steve.

Steve's trial was reported in every newspaper and on every TV news bulletin. And from those background reports I learned things about my husband I had never known. I had always wondered whether Steve had truly loved Trish, whether he had been a different man then. Sometimes I suspected that Trish had worn the trousers in their relationship and he took out all his pent-up frustrations on me. I was crediting him with the feelings of a normal person, yet Steve was clearly and disturbingly abnormal. According to the *Daily Mirror*, 'Wilson, it has emerged, terrorised his own parents – holding a knife to his mother's throat when he was 15. His first wife Trisha died of cancer, aged 33, in 1992. A family friend said, "You could call it a merciful release.'"

On 27 March 2003, the day Steve was sentenced to two life terms with no chance of parole, a man called Keith Young took his four beautiful blond boys to a beauty spot in Wales and killed them in his car. He attached a pipe to a lawnmower in the boot of his car and, all the while giving his estranged wife a running commentary from his mobile phone, turned on the engine and gassed the boys, who were aged between seven and three. Two hours earlier, he'd called his wife to say he would harm the kids.

I'll never be sure if Keith, who also took his own life that day, had copied Steve after reading what he'd done in court reports but it hit me terribly hard. I blame myself and have carried the guilt of that, and of every single one of those despicable crimes, ever since then.

Chapter 24
Tabloid Truths

Kevin and I talked about trying to push Steve out of our minds and focusing fully on the future together. Because, despite his sentence, I could not fully believe that Steve would never be set loose to terrorise me again.

'What if he gets out, Kevin? The first thing he'll do is find me and kill me. And you. And what if he tried to get to Owen?'

'Dee, there's no way he will get out, love. The judge said he can't apply for parole. The jury unanimously found him guilty so, even if he tries to appeal, they'll say the same.'

But I still couldn't be sure. 'I think we should move house. He could easily track us down here. Let's move really far away – let's live abroad.'

Kevin was adamant we should stand our ground and that Steve would not rule my life with fear any longer.

'We won't let him drive us out of our house, we will stay where we are,' he told me.

I knew that, if Steve came to our house, Kevin would have stood in his way and not budged even if it meant that Steve killed him – Kevin was that kind of man.

Even though Steve was finally behind bars, I looked over my shoulder for him wherever I went. I wouldn't get into my car in the dark because I worried he'd be crouched down in the back seat, waiting to pounce. And I was too scared to go out with Owen on my own. Even if I was with Kevin in Tesco buying nappies, I felt sure he would jump out from behind the shelves and grab me. The sight of security cameras was always reassuring because I knew they could be shown in court. But then again, they'd be no use to me if I was dead. I preferred staying in with Owen and made all sorts of excuses not to go out.

It sounded an illogical fear to most but no one could understand just how devious Steve could be. I knew that, if anyone could escape from a maximum security prison, he could.

He had once had his car impounded by the police for driving offences but he broke into the police pound and drove his car away. And if he could kill his own kids, whom he was meant to love and protect to the ends of the earth, he would easily kill a police officer or prison guard. That's why, even though I was thoroughly exhausted looking after Owen, I could hardly ever sleep in those early days after the verdict.

On the rare occasions Kevin and I did go out, a steady stream of well-meaning people would come up to us to say, 'I'm sorry for your loss' and 'He got what he deserved'. I thanked them and was grateful for so much support. It was a comfort to know that so many people felt moved that my boys were no longer here but I always resisted expressing an inner voice that said, 'Steve didn't get what he deserved. Letting me do to him what he did to my boys would be real justice.'

Even though Steve had committed the heinous crime, I always felt ashamed and embarrassed when people who knew my story approached me. I knew it meant they had closely followed media reports of the trial. And that also meant they knew I had worked as a prostitute.

All I could do was try to be as humble, polite and friendly as I could so they could judge for themselves if I was a brazen whore or a mum manipulated by a cruel and murderous control freak. I hoped seeing Kevin by my side was a sign that maybe I wasn't worthless and was worth loving.

I couldn't take each person aside and explain that Steve would have killed me if I hadn't had sex with other men to earn him money. It wasn't exactly socially acceptable to reveal to the strangers who approached me all the gory details of my hellish 10 years at his evil hands. But I wanted to. I had an urgent and burning need to clear my name as publicly as it was trashed during the trial. So, when Amanda told me the *News of the World* wanted to do an exclusive two-page interview with me to get my side of the story across, I agreed.

Dealing with the press was a surreal experience. At the boys' funeral cameras clicked as soon as I stepped out of the car and I could hear people in the crowd tut-tutting and saying, 'Look at those vultures. Leave her alone.'

Every day courier cars and taxis turned up at Mum's house, and later Kevin's house too, to deliver letters and contracts from magazines and TV stations asking for interviews. After the trial the press interest revved up to a higher gear. All the attention was the last thing I needed – it was like having a taste of the downside of being famous.

Amanda screened all the calls from the media. I chose to speak to the *News of the World* because all my friends read it and it was the paper with the biggest reach. Clearing my name was vital, as was telling the truth of my story to try to convince other women in abusive relationships to leave. The £10,500 fee would help me and Kevin with all the costs of looking after Owen and his three kids, as I hadn't worked since the boys' deaths and wanted to contribute. Amanda did all the negotiations and, before she agreed on my behalf, she researched the work of the journalist Paul Lewis and got sincere assurances that he would treat me and my story sensitively.

On the way to do the interview at the Hyatt Hotel in Birmingham, the *Sunday People* rang Amanda's phone and offered a £20,000 fee. But speaking to the newspapers wasn't about the money – it was about letting the widest possible audience hear my side of the story. I declined the offer.

The *News of the World* had promised to look after me and they definitely did. The interview was held in the hotel's presidential suite, which was bigger than my house. The bed was the size of three doubles, there was a Jacuzzi, living room and even a kitchen there.

The journalist Paul Lewis was gentle with his questioning. Amanda wouldn't have let him be anything less. I was completely open and honest with my answers because by then I had nothing to hide.

Owen was with us throughout and having him there really helped get me through the process of re-telling all the horrible experiences with Steve. Just looking at cute little Owen, in his tiny little beige chinos, tank top and navy shoes, was a real-life reminder that I was talking to the media to help look after my family so I had to keep going and be strong.

It was Mother's Day, five days after the verdict, and I was struggling without Bret and Brad Lee. I missed being woken by them bringing me a bowl of mushy cornflakes in bed, spilling half of them along the hallway, and thrusting them under my nose while singing, 'Happy Mother's Day to you'.

I missed their proud little faces when they presented me with their homemade cards, usually with flowers or a smiley face felt-penned on the front and with big blobs of still-tacky glue and inky fingerprints as testament to the effort they'd put in. Their Mother's Day presents had been daffodils they'd picked from the park and bound with a red elastic band, which the postman dropped on the pavements. Sometimes their gifts were promises that they'd tidy their rooms 'all day long'.

Steve would have known that getting through that day without them would have been particularly hard for me. Kevin knew it too, which is why he brought me breakfast and the Sunday papers in bed, with little Owen tucked under his arm. It was a lovely gesture that made me smile and brush away the tears that fell as soon as I woke.

It was so strange to pick up a newspaper and see my own face alongside smiling pictures of Bret and Brad Lee on holiday. Under the headline 'MUM OF CHILDREN BUTCHERED BY DAD TELLS HOW HER WORLD FELL APART', I told the nation my truthful account of falling into Steve's clutches at 16, being beaten by him and my humiliation and revulsion at being forced into prostitution. The story described how I saw the look of terror on Bret and Brad Lee's faces when Steve killed them in my nightmares and how the fear they felt would never leave me. I was so pleased that it included my ambition to become a counsellor for battered women and a warning: 'Nothing will ever replace my babies. But if I can stop this sort of thing happening to one other person then at least something positive has happened. Men like Steve will never change and the longer you stay the harder it is to leave. Don't wait until it's too late.'

I wish that story hadn't been about me. I wish I didn't have a 'shocking exclusive' to tell and didn't have to represent a worst-case scenario for other abused women. But at least – and at last – my voice would be heard.

On the same day my story appeared, the *Sunday People* carried an interview with Konrad. Unbeknown to each other, we had both told our stories of life with Steve in newspapers published on the same day.

The headline on Konrad's story ran: 'MY HELL WITH EVIL SCREWDRIVER DAD; HE MADE ME EAT DEAD MUM'S ASHES, TRIED TO MAKE ME COMMIT SUICIDE AND SLASHED MY NECK WITH A MACHETE'. He showed his machete scar in the pictures and in his interview branded Steve a monster who did not deserve a breath of fresh air for the rest of his life. Unfortunately, as I could testify, it was all true.

The article told me details I'd never known of Steve's brutal treatment of Konrad, Stacey and even Trish. Konrad said Steve had ruled with an iron fist but that Trish had always shielded them from his drunken rages. When Trish died of cancer aged 33, Steve forced him at the age of 13 to help put Trish's body in the coffin. He later made Konrad and Stacey pose in front of the open coffin at the funeral parlour while he photographed them.

Konrad said he dared not refuse because he knew the beatings would begin.

At the crematorium Konrad told how Steve defied staff and forced him and Stacey to watch their mother's coffin enter the furnace. He described how he and Stacey cried their eyes out watching it burn while Steve took photographs of it all because he said it was important that they saw it happen. Then there was a bombshell about the mysterious source of Steve's income. Konrad said Steve needed drinking money because he had blown Trish's £42,000 life insurance in a year on cars and holidays. He described how Steve had taught him to play pool and made him skip school to play for money. He would win £20 here and there to buy Steve's rum. But if Konrad lost, Steve would stay calm until they got home then beat him across the face. Konrad told how Steve made him move into the garden shed and charged him £60 a week even in cold winters.

Konrad explained that he was only allowed into the house to babysit for Bret and Brad. He said Steve had pressured him to marry Gemma and live together in the shed, and how Gemma had rebelled against his tyranny and left with Loren.

Konrad's story included Steve's threats to hunt him down and kill him if he left home. And he detailed a horrific attack after Gemma left when he was playing pool with his dad. He said, 'I was about to take a shot when he grabbed his cue like a baseball bat and smashed it into my face.' When Konrad had asked why he'd been hit, Steve laughed. Konrad likened his dad to a dog that turns on you for no reason.

Konrad also revealed something shocking I hadn't known, possibly because it happened at a time when I was at a women's refuge. In 1999, Steve had urged him to commit suicide when he could take no more and so he had swallowed paracetamol. Konrad said Steve had laughed and goaded him by saying, 'You were always a loser. Go on, kill yourself.' Stacey had called an ambulance and Konrad recovered after three days.

To think Steve almost killed all three of his sons.

I felt sorry for Konrad and Stacey. And I was glad Konrad had told his story because I hope it meant he got support from people around him. Our memories of life with Steve were so dark they sounded too bleak to be real. He was so barbaric that our accurate reports of him seemed far-fetched. People must have thought, 'Surely he wasn't that bad? Surely no one could treat their family so despicably?' But they could, and he did.

Although I'd gained a new, and black, insight into Konrad's life, I still didn't want to get in contact with him. I understand he was his dad's puppet. But his father killed my kids. Although it made no sense, I couldn't help looking for someone to blame so, to prevent me saying unjust things to Konrad, I chose to stay away.

Reading those stories on such an emotional morning made me feel stronger that we'd finally got the whole truth out there, we'd won the last word from Steve and I'd cleared my name. Then I read another newspaper and sank lower than I had in months.

In the *Sunday Mirror*, columnist Carole Malone had her say about me. I am sure Carole is a perfectly lovely lady, and I know that it is her job to be controversial to stir up reaction among readers, but reading her words on Mother's Day without my eldest sons hurt more than any of Steve's beatings.

Carole said, 'While I have boundless sympathy for the victims of cruel and sustained domestic violence, what the hell did Denise Wilson think she was doing leaving those kids, aged just seven and eight, with a man she knew to be a monster? She knew he was violent.

'Yet still she walked out, leaving little Brad Lee and Bret at his mercy.'

She went on to say that only a mother who doesn't love her kids enough would walk away. And that, although Steve might be guilty of murder, I was guilty of something that would haunt the rest of my life.

My stomach tightened and eyes filled as I read each damning word. By the time I'd reached the final paragraph, I was speechless with pain and guilt. I could imagine the millions of readers, the fellow mums also having breakfast in bed with the papers, nodding in agreement and judging me as the world's worst mother without knowing or understanding my full story. And right then I wanted to die.

The last time I'd reached rock bottom Kevin was there to catch my hand and help support me to stand up again. And, as if he had a sixth sense, he did exactly the same again. Because after leaving me on my own in peace with the newspapers for an hour, he came back into our bedroom with Owen on his hip, dropped to one knee and said, 'I haven't got a ring yet, but I have never loved anyone as much as I love you. I have never felt this way before. Denise, will you do me the honour of marrying me?'

Chapter 25
Safe At Last

I was stunned. Looking at Kevin down on his knee, with a nervous little smile, promised positivity and hope in my life: I had him and Owen to live for. I knew I would be happy and secure with Kevin so I said yes to his proposal. Or rather, I squeaked yes.

Kevin looked absolutely delighted. He climbed into bed and he, Owen and I had a huge cuddle. I didn't bring up how the words of a columnist in a national newspaper had just left me feeling as if I'd been winded by a punch to the stomach. We didn't talk about rings, dates, weddings, honeymoons or any of that frivolous stuff. We just held each other and said over and over again 'I love you so much'. I could not wait to be Kevin's wife, felt proud that he would be my husband and could scarcely believe that such a good man had come into my life to save me from such a bad time.

Our engagement came so soon after the trauma of the trial that we knew people would disapprove. But I'd been condemned so many times it was time to give up trying to please everyone.

I had grown used to people seeing me coming, turning their backs and holding their hands up to their mouths in a ridiculous attempt to hide the fact they were talking about me. My morals and motivation had been torn to pieces in that column that day. But getting engaged to Kevin made me feel happy and secure. It helped beam another light of optimism into my future; I hoped no one would deny me that.

My experiences with the men in my life had been cruel and cold, but whenever Kevin held me I felt swaddled in warmth. Owen helped me, too. Life had been hard, but whenever I held him I felt nothing but softness.

I had never read pregnancy or baby books before the birth of Bret and Brad Lee because I'd never had time to relax or concentrate on me. Life was so much more laid-back with Kevin so I read piles of books before Owen's birth. Expert authors said babies pick up on their mother's moods but I didn't have a sad or stressed baby: Owen didn't inherit my anxiety, he was a little dream. It was as if he just knew how to mend Mummy's broken heart by being a placid, easy-to-please happy soul. I was so glad he was mine and that I was still a mum on Mother's Day.

Kevin's proposal, and the feeling of gratitude I had for Owen's very existence, made me resolve from that moment on that nothing and no one would burst our happy little family bubble.

At around 1.30pm, Manny, a police liaison officer who worked with Amanda, rang my mobile. I knew it was Steve-related so passed Owen to Kevin and went out into the garden to take the call.

Manny said, 'I don't know if I should class this as good or bad news but Steve is dead. He was found hanging in his cell.'

I was silent for a few seconds as I struggled to absorb the news.

'He's really dead? Honestly? Has his body been checked by a doctor?'

He was such a monster, and so conniving, I wouldn't have put it past Steve to play dead so he could later jump off the mortuary slab and escape through the morgue doors.

'Yes, Denise – he is absolutely dead. He was found hanging from his bootlaces from an upturned bed in his cell.'

I punched the air. It was true, Steve was finally gone. Immediately the atmosphere outside seemed fresher, purer.

I walked back inside to tell Kevin but didn't need to.

'Steve's dead, isn't he?' he said.

'Yes. How did you know?'

'I could see the joy in your face.'

Kevin gave me a long, tight hug then picked up Owen so the three of us could have another family embrace.

Finally, we were all safe.

On the surface, it seems inevitable that Steve would kill himself rather than serve a life sentence in jail. First of all, he was a coward. He would not have been able to withstand the harsh prison environment and couldn't have coped with not being kingpin among the other inmates. Secondly, he had an extreme aversion to authority so, if a judge said he would have to live the rest of his life in jail, Steve would have said, 'Screw you – I don't have to suffer this.' He would rather have ended his life than endured it behind bars just to spite the judge, just to flick two fingers up to the entire justice system and me. He knew that it's the prison officers' duty to prevent inmates committing suicide and so he would have enjoyed the thought of getting them into trouble. Most of all, it was vital to him to retain ultimate control, right to the very end.

But look deeper into the demonic inner workings of Steve and, to me, it's clear that there was no way he would take his own life. He had the perfect opportunity to do that when he was in the car with my boys but he didn't have the guts. He knew how to kill – he had done it twice. When the police search helicopter was overhead, he kept telling Konrad on the phone that he couldn't find his heart to stab it – so why on earth didn't he just cut his own left carotid artery? For years he had lectured us about how it was the quickest way to kill. Fact is, he didn't do it because he was just too scared.

That's why I have a strong instinct that Steve died in his cell because other prisoners got to him. As a double child killer, he would never have made any allies and always been a target. He was too arrogant to keep a low profile in prison. And he was too big to hang from shoelaces tied to the end of an upturned bed. Besides, if he was going to commit suicide why didn't he do it on the first night after the guilty verdict?

I am not a violent person – I abhor any kind of violence. But I make an exception for violence against Steve. I hope he screamed and cried in fear as he realised he was taking his last choked breaths. And I hope he spent his last moments being called all the despicable names he had earned when he took my sons' lives.

I will never know for sure if Steve's suicide was just that or if it was an 'assisted' suicide. But the fact was that he was finally gone from this earth and was now burning in hell.

Now I could breathe again. I could go out without freezing in terror at the sight of men with roughly the same height, build or tight curly hair. He could never be behind me at the traffic lights, could never break the front door down.

I could sleep again. I need never lie awake, sweating and rigid with fear, in case the creak I'd heard was him creeping up the stairs ready to knife me, Kevin and our baby. Now I was safe in the knowledge that the rustling sound from the garden would never be Steve sneaking out from his hiding place armed with knives and enough aggression to slay an entire family.

The relief was so enormous it left me shattered. A decade of tension eased away.

But grief for my sons, the urgent yearning for them, didn't go away so after a few days I felt angry. Because Steve's not suffering now, is he? He deserved to suffer more, to slowly rot away.

When victims' families give statements outside court, they often say it's the people left behind and not the criminals who serve the life sentence. It's said so often that it's a cliché but it's

said because it is painfull̲y̲ [text obscured]
I could never have what *I* d[text obscured]

In newspaper reports, [text obscured] 'apparent suicide'. Police author[text obscured] investigation into why he wasn't p[text obscured] not sure I ever heard the outcome of [text obscured] sure I ever need to.

My divorce hadn't come through by [text obscured] Steve died. Officially, I was his next of kin but I am so glad the authorities used their common sense rather than protocol and no one contacted me to identify his body. There was no way I'd have done it – no way I wanted to ever see his hateful face again, dead or alive.

And so his corpse lay rotting on a mortuary slab without anyone claiming his disgusting body for four days. In the end, he had to be identified by the Prison Service, who matched the fingerprints to their records.

The *Birmingham Evening Mail* reported that Steve would have a pauper's grave and I felt this was fitting but at the last minute an anonymous donor paid the £213 fee for a no-frills burial.

I believe the secret benefactor must have been either Konrad or Steve's younger brother Martin because they were the only two reported to have turned up at the cemetery. The paper said both arrived in casual clothes and left five minutes later. Stacey didn't turn up, nor did Steve's parents. He was buried in the cheapest coffin available and no flowers were left, no wake was held.

anyone who would be so detested by his
even in death. The indignity of being buried not
your family but near your prison was exactly what Steve
deserved. He was so hung up on status that I like to think he
was spinning in that grave – that pauper's grave.

Konrad refused to speak to the newspaper reporter at the
cemetery but Martin said, 'It is finished and done now. I felt it
was my place to finish it. It has come to an end now.'

And so it had finally come to an end for me, too. Only now
that I knew he was buried did I finally believe Steve was truly
dead. My nightmare, my decade of fear and horror at his giant
murderous hands, was over.

I desperately wanted to permanently delete Steve from our
life but still had some of his affairs to tidy up. Since I was still
legally married to him when he died, I assumed the house at
Linden Avenue would automatically go to me. But I was wrong.
Even though I had paid the mortgage for years, Steve never put
my name on the mortgage papers. In fact, Trish's name was still
on them.

Since Steve's imprisonment, no one had paid the mortgage
so the house was about to be repossessed. My solicitor advised
me to sell it for cash as quickly as I could.

Kevin came with me when I returned to the house to collect
the only things I wanted from there, which were Bret and Brad
Lee's belongings. I kept their baby photographs, their favourite
teddies, their folders of school work and their favourite toys,

which were mini computers called Palm Powers that helped the boys with spelling, sums, reading and logic. I gave their clothes to charity so they could live on, in a way. And I found those super-sharp scissors that had sliced into Steve's arm and cut his clothes into tiny pieces.

It was gut-wrenching to be back at that house again, yet more peaceful than it had been on the day of the boys' funerals. Since Steve was dead, I thought less of my hatred for him and more of the day I brought my baby sons home from hospital here, the cuddles we'd shared, the laughs we had rather than the beatings I'd withstood. I cried for my boys, torn away from me so traumatically, but I knew I never needed to be back there: the history of the house was too bloody, the memories too sad.

Within weeks, a man who lived nearby bought the house for £10,000 and all I had to do was write a letter confirming that the property now belonged to the new owner. But I had certain conditions attached to the sale.

'I want nothing else to do with this house. I don't want to see any paperwork; I don't want any follow-up calls, nothing. I just want to walk away and never look back.'

'Deal.'

And he *did* get a deal because two years later the house was re-sold for £95,000. I looked at the pictures on the estate agent's website, which felt weird – as if I was peering into my old front window. The stairs I was thrown down were ripped out and replaced with a stylish metal spiral staircase. Some of the downstairs walls I was pinned up against had been knocked through to create an airy open-plan layout. The floor I'd bled on had been covered with smart new laminate and the bathroom where I'd discovered and lost pregnancies was all new and unrecognisable. But the site didn't show the boys' room – the only room I wanted to see. It was the only bedroom they had ever known, it was their world and was meant to be where they felt safest of all. It was where I'd left them.

I genuinely hope that whoever lives there now helps change the historical pattern of that house and is truly happy. But I never want to see that house again. With Steve and his house both gone, it was time to close the door and move on.

Chapter 26

A Fresh Start

Life changed so much after Steve's death and all for the better. I still thought about Bret and Brad Lee every day but my thoughts of them had more clarity now my mind wasn't so befuddled with memories of trials, revenge or brutality. Now I could focus more on Kevin, Owen and making life as happy as it could be for us all.

I'd spent a decade fearing Steve and far too long wasting energy hating him. It had been hell for us all. But I've always believed that you get out of life what you put into it. And I wanted to put everything I could into my new life with Kevin and Owen because I knew I was lucky to have them.

Kevin was the polar opposite of Steve. A strong man who never needed to dominate and didn't live in a world of falsehoods and fantasy, he was gentlemanly and his top priority in life was making me and Owen feel loved and secure. Somehow he just knew whenever emotional or domestic life was getting a bit much for me and would send me off to bed, making promises I knew he would keep of looking after Owen while I slept. Whenever I was feeling maudlin, Kevin would listen to me for hours, saying all the right things, which were ultimately 'everything will be all right'.

And he was a doting daddy. He changed Owen's nappies, bathed him, winded him and was always happy to do his feeds, even though they both ended up covered head-to-toe in baby mush. Kevin delighted in Owen. In fact, he could barely be a few steps away from his baby son. If I put Owen in his crib for a nap I'd see him snuggled into Kevin's chest half an hour later, still asleep but there just because Kevin wanted to be close and sing soft little nursery rhymes to him.

'Kevin, leave Owen in his crib – you're spoiling him.'

'Sorry, he just jumped out of his crib and into my arms.'

Living with Dave Angel and then Steve gave me the impression that all men were wired to get blind drunk as often as they could but Kevin wasn't like that. If ever he was at the club he was watching football or playing snooker, not necking pints as if his life depended on it. He never drank in the house and even if he did have a few beers at the pub he was never belligerent, never showed even a tiniest hint of aggression. Instead, booze made him a bit chattier before he'd take himself off to bed. He enjoyed peace and quiet but was never more content than when he was with me and Owen.

I, on the other hand, was not easy to live with. In fact, I was a nightmare. My mood swings were dramatic and tantrums spectacular. I had a personal rule book and made it clear that I'd have zero tolerance if anyone overstepped the mark.

Kevin was never allowed to raise his voice to me, never mind his hand. And he was not permitted to keep any financial detail or control from me. I would never let him order me around.

There really was no need for such rules as Kevin wasn't the type of man who would ever want to verbally, physically or financially abuse me but in those early days together just being able to set those boundaries made me feel better.

If ever Kevin and I disagreed, one of us would walk away. Neither of us would ever let an argument get so out of hand that it escalated to shouting or screaming. I felt awful after any fallout with Kevin but because he knew exactly what I'd been through he understood where my moods came from.

'Nobody's perfect,' he always said when we made up. 'If everyone was perfect we'd live in a boring world.'

Money was always tight. I received sickness benefits because my doctor classed me as depressed. Despite the diagnosis, I refused to take anti-depressant pills again. I had taken them for a short time just after the boys had been killed and didn't want any more. I know they help a great many people and in no way judge anyone who needs or takes them but I worried that if I'd have taken them my mind would have realised I had a problem and cracked up. Mentally, I worked really hard to stay on top of things and didn't want to risk altering that.

But I still felt depressed. I still tortured myself with guilt that I was moving on with my life yet Bret and Brad Lee couldn't move on with theirs. And I still cried about my boys every day but after a while I'd think, 'Why am I crying when I have a lovely family to look after?' I told myself I was lucky to be here, fortunate to have Kevin and Owen. I'd remind myself there were people far worse off than me and my thoughts turned to Keith Young's widow, Samantha Tolley, who lost her four beautiful boys. Four, that's absolutely mind blowing.

I had to do everything I could for women like Samantha and to prevent others from having a terrible story like ours. I had a fierce ambition to try to help those in similar situations, but with a young baby and no experience or qualifications in counselling I knew this would be difficult. Instead, all I could do was try to tell my story to as many people as possible in the hope that it would serve as a warning.

I asked Amanda to accept an invitation to be interviewed on ITV's *This Morning* in the week after the verdict so I could try to reach out to its millions of viewers. As always, she was right beside me in the green room and stayed there until the cameras counted down to my live interview. I was always grateful for Amanda's support but wasn't a bit nervous despite the daunting surroundings of a studio. Living through everything I'd endured with Steve meant I was now scared of nothing and no one.

The show's presenters Fern Britton and Phillip Schofield were as friendly, warm and empathetic in real life as they are on screen and made me feel very welcome and relaxed. I told them as much as I could about my years of hell with Steve in the hope that somewhere in the country a viewer would recognise that she was living with the same pattern of abuse and might gather the strength to leave. Every person I met in the *This Morning* studio was lovely and they even sent me a beautiful bouquet of flowers afterwards to thank me for coming on the show.

I also appeared on *The Jeremy Kyle Show* to do a special episode featuring me in a one-to-one with Jeremy and following a very different format to the riotous 'my husband slept with my best friend' episodes. I surprised myself by not feeling intimidated by the studio audience or Jeremy as I sat in the spotlight on stage. The audience was absolutely silent as Jeremy led me through my story. Again, I urged women to try to recognise the personality traits of control, possessiveness and aggression that Steve had in spades and to run for the hills. I will never know if my message resonated even with just one viewer, but knowing that I'd tried my very best to help them helped me feel more positive about myself.

Not long after the TV appearances I met a young woman who was a living embodiment of the message that leaving a destructive relationship saves lives. Kevin and I were shopping in Sutton Coldfield when I heard someone say, 'Hello, Dee.' I glanced back, saw the face of someone I didn't recognise and said a vague 'hello' back. Since losing the boys, my memory had deteriorated, so I asked Kevin, 'Who was that?' His answer made me stop in my tracks, turn back and hug her, 'It was Gemma.'

'*Gemma!*'

I had not seen her since the disastrous evening at the blues bar. And I would never have recognised her now. The back-combed,

Trish-style curly hair was now sleek and straight and she looked far more confident, sophisticated and self-composed. She was a strong young woman and no longer the little nervous teen Steve liked to bully and beat.

For a while, we did not know what to say and just held each other. We both cried as she sympathised with the loss of Bret and Brad Lee and we reminisced about the two wonderful boys who had brightened up a black time for us both.

'I'm so sorry about what happened to Bret and Brad Lee,' Gemma said.

'But I am so glad you left when you did,' I said.

Gemma explained that she did receive the note I left at her flat but was terrified it was a ploy by Steve to entice her from her hiding place. She imagined Steve standing over my shoulder as I wrote it and circling her tower block of flats in his Daihatsu. That was a very realistic thought and I completely understood why she was too scared to respond to the letter.

Gemma said, 'I am so sorry, Dee. As soon as I heard what Steve did to your boys I was devastated. You've no idea how guilty I feel for not listening to your cry for help.'

'Don't think about it like that,' I told her. 'You're right, if I had moved in with you, Steve might very well have found us all. I don't resent you for it and don't blame you at all.'

We didn't have time to say everything we needed to say on the street so Gemma and I swapped phone numbers. I was glad to hear she had a new relationship and was happily working, but upset to learn that she had suffered a nervous breakdown for a full year after escaping from Linden Avenue.

She was too scared to leave her flat because she feared Steve would be waiting for her in that blasted green Daihatsu. Just a glimpse of a green car on the road sent her into a panic. She suffered severe paranoia that had to be treated with prescription pills.

The emotional collapse left Gemma so stricken her dad had to look after baby Loren during this time. She and her father had applied for joint custody so that, with Gemma too unwell to look after Loren full-time, her dad could give consent for any medical treatment Loren might need. Counselling had helped piece together her shattered soul and get her back on her feet.

In a way, it was a comfort to us both to have someone else to talk to who had endured those years because the details of life with Steve were so horrific that they sound unbelievable to anyone who wasn't there. We had survived traumatic times together, which had formed personality traits we both shared. Having been so victimised, so downtrodden and belittled we were now fazed by nothing and filled with a ferocious need to protect our kids. We promised not to lose touch and to help pick each other up whenever we needed it.

Gemma was thrilled that I had found love with Kevin, whom she'd known from all the times Steve forced her and Konrad to drink with him at the Old Oscott club. We re-formed a solid friendship and I was delighted to see that Loren had grown into a beautiful, bright and loving little girl. Although Gemma was still legally married to Konrad, they hadn't spoken since the night she fled the cabin. Loren had no contact with her dad.

Seeing how far Gemma had come in life further inspired me to get on with my own. I knew I could sit in a corner and cry all day and that everyone would have understood but I am not that kind of person. Even as a child I rarely felt sorry for myself. So I stopped going to the doctor for sick notes and in so doing stopped my sickness benefits. And when Owen was eight months old I went back out to work.

Gemma had a word with her boss at a small cleaning firm and they took me on. And I loved it. We worked in teams of two and I enjoyed the company of the other women. It felt good to be out earning an honest living for my family. Even if it wasn't the most glamorous of occupations, I enjoyed it. I liked being in big posh houses with expensive glass ornaments and imagining where I'd put my furniture if I lived there. Having my hand down someone else's loo was a million times better than what Steve had made me do. I think I earned around £8 an hour, not the £100 from Sensations, but I was proud of every pound.

The distraction of work, and the knowledge that I was no longer on benefits, really helped me. Working hard was part of my coping process because I was too busy to sit around stewing. Leaving Owen at home was the downside. I was naturally distrustful of leaving my baby son with anyone, and given what I'd been through I could also have felt uneasy leaving him with

Kevin. But I had seen the way Kevin was with his own three kids. I knew that nothing made him lose his temper and I trusted him implicitly.

Kevin and I worked our shifts around each other so one of us was always with our son. Even then I called Kevin every hour to check on Owen and insisted he put the phone to him just so I could hear him gurgle, or even just breathe. There was no way I could ever have left Owen with a childminder. God no. I didn't want him to be out of his home environment. At first, I didn't want to leave him at all, ever, but I knew I had to trust some people with my child or else I shouldn't have had any more children.

Kevin and I became even closer the more time we spent together. It felt good to be working together to solidify the foundations of a new family life. That also involved building bridges with my mum, sisters and even Dave.

My feelings toward Dave didn't exactly warm, but as he got older he mellowed and became less bolshie and opinionated. I couldn't be bothered waging a war against him, I didn't have the energy to bear grudges. What happened to Bret and Brad Lee made me realise how short life is and so, although memories of his mistreatment of me and my two elder sisters as young kids never went away, in my mid-twenties I felt it was time to establish a new relationship. And Dave was probably scared to upset me because he'd have faced the wrath of the rest of the family.

Despite our losing contact during the Steve years, my relationship with my sisters picked up where we left off and we all got on well. Angie lived around the corner. Nicky was still living at home with Mum and her sons, Ben and Liam, and helped me an awful lot, especially in the early days after losing the boys. Amy was also still at home and loved helping me look after Owen, while Sarah lived not too far away with her partner, Paul, and their pretty little daughter, Chloe.

My family grew to know and love Kevin, too. On the day he bought me my gold engagement ring with a white stone, Mum said, 'I am so pleased for you – it's lovely to see you happy again. You've found the right one this time.'

Everything about being with Kevin felt right. He was teaching me that I could trust my own judgement, that I deserved to be treated with love, care and consideration. He was the backbone of the secure family I had always craved. And so, even though we kept our engagement pretty low profile, I was thrilled to be Kevin's fiancée.

This time I would not have a shotgun wedding with strangers as witnesses and a reception in a crappy pub. This time we would have the works.

Chapter 27
A Birth, Marriage And Death Knell

Kevin and I married on my birthday, 16 July 2005. It was my dream wedding and a day when I'd never felt so special.

We had both decided we'd been through so much that we wanted to truly celebrate finding each other and falling in love. We had formed a new and mutual circle of friends and wanted everyone together to share our special day so we really pushed the boat out.

It was important for us to have a church wedding, but because Kevin was divorced we knew not every church would marry us. But after a meeting with Martin Rutter, the vicar of St Margaret's Church in Great Barr, he agreed to conduct our marriage service. He was a lovely man and we were delighted.

I asked Dave Angel to give me away. Not to show that we had found a deep love and respect for each other, or to pretend that he'd been a great father figure, but to keep Mum happy and also to keep the peace. Dave seemed surprised but chuffed. He went as far as his suit fitting before he said, 'I can't do this,' and backed out of giving me away. I was let down by Dave yet again but didn't want to start a family war afresh and just thought about finding someone else for the job. It was obvious there was a special someone who had guided me through life and given me unstinting support: Amanda.

'I've never been asked to be a father-of-the-bride before,' she said, 'but I'd be honoured.'

I bought Mum a beautiful mother-of-the-bride suit with a long jacket and skirt in pale blue. I loved being able to do that for her because I'd worked hard and saved the money.

On the morning of the wedding, Dave went fishing before the ceremony, so as the only other driver in the family I drove to the house to pick up Mum and my sisters and take them back to Kevin's so we could all get ready together. Kevin stayed at his mum's house because everyone knows it's bad luck to see the bride on the morning of the wedding – and Lord knows, we did not need any bad luck.

It was a scorching hot day when the sunshine amplified all the colours of the flowers to technicolour. I couldn't wait to get into my dress: it was white silk and had a lace heart on the back and a six-foot train. As soon as I saw it, I had to have it. I had booked a nice big church and wanted a nice big dress to wear there. It was stunning – no one would ever have known it was from a charity shop. Amanda turned up early with a bottle of champagne. She did my make-up beautifully and helped me get into my dress.

By then I was working as an assistant in a hair salon, doing shampoos and rinsing off colours. The girls from the salon gave me the full VIP treatment. They piled my hair high and left ringlets loose, which made me look and feel really glamorous, and the girls refused to take payment for it. It was so kind of them and I felt amazing.

As soon as Mum saw me she cried.

'At last, babby,' she said, 'you are finally happy. After everything you have been through, here you are, looking like a princess with your family around you and a good man waiting for you at the church. I am so proud of you, Dee.'

Of course, all my family couldn't be with me. It was yet another day when I wished I could borrow Bret and Brad Lee from Heaven, even just for a few minutes. But the boys were close to me, in a way. The most important part of my outfit was the gold heart-shaped locket around my neck, which was a gift from Kevin's mum and had pictures of Bret and Brad Lee inside. How I longed for them to have been more than just a picture that day.

Gemma was my maid of honour and my sister Sarah's little girl, Chloe, was a flower girl. Owen was two-and-a-half and looked absolutely adorable in a teensy page boy's black suit with silk lapels, which he wore with a burgundy dickie bow on elastic.

We hired a limousine to take Kevin to the church then swing back to pick me up. The limo company also sent a Mercedes with ribbons on for free because the wedding before ours had finished early. That was such a lovely gesture and meant more guests could arrive in chauffeured style.

As the limo approached the church, the George Michael cover of Paul McCartney's song 'The Long and Winding Road' played on the stereo, which seemed wholly appropriate because it was a long and winding road to the church. Everything felt perfect. But as soon as our posh car drew to a stop, I got a serious bout of the jitters.

'I can't do this,' I said to Amanda, refusing to get out of the car because my legs felt too weak to hold me up.

'It's just nerves, Denise. You *can* do it. Come on.'

She was always so good at talking me into feeling stronger.

As I stood at the top of the aisle and heard the excited murmurs of our 150 guests, I wasn't sure if I could make it down. Thoughts of Bret and Brad Lee's funeral swam around in my head and again I felt guilty for moving on without them. Amanda had to remind me, in a whisper, that my memories of Bret and Brad Lee wouldn't go away just because I was getting married.

I walked down the aisle on Amanda's arm to the sound of the organist playing classical wedding music and as soon as I saw Kevin's smile all nerves vanished.

'You look beautiful,' he said. And right then I felt it. After that moment it seemed as if just Kevin and I were standing alone in that beautiful church – we didn't take our eyes off each other.

The vicar had assured us that it didn't matter if we fluffed our lines, so, when he fluffed his, we both had a fit of giggles.

I felt overwhelmed with happiness when we were proclaimed husband and wife; I'd never experienced feeling so loved.

When we walked hand in hand back up the aisle and out into the blazing sunshine, I felt as if my heart was singing along to the sound of our wedding bells. Ten minutes of those bells cost us £80 but they were worth every penny because the jubilant celebratory sound of them echoed our feelings.

Owen had done his best to steal my thunder during the service by picking the flowers in the church and then running up and down the aisle until the vicar had to chase after him. He was naughty because my sister Amy had looked after him while I was getting ready, and because she's so soft on kids she couldn't leave him in his cot for a nap because he cried. It didn't really matter in the end because the guests thought his cheeky behaviour was hilarious.

We all really let our hair down at the reception, which we held at a working men's club called The Warriors. Early that morning, my sister Angie and I had decorated it with balloons and heart-shaped paper decorations.

Amanda's speech was so lovely it made me cry. She said she had known me for a few years and sadly met me through the deaths of Bret and Brad Lee, adding that she was glad to know me because I had been a strong inspiration to her and even helped her through a few problems of her own. At the end she said, 'Please raise your glasses to Kevin and Denise, and Bret and Brad Lee.' It was a lovely touch and brought my two lost boys into the forefront of our guests' minds and tears to our eyes.

Kevin chose the music for our first dance, which was 'You Make Me Feel Brand New' by The Stylistics. The lyrics were perfectly apt.

As we twirled around the dance floor I felt giddy with happiness.

Mum was at our wedding reception for only 10 minutes before Dave insisted it was time to go home. She said, 'Dee, I'm ever so sorry – I didn't know he would want to go so early.' By then I had a new insight into Mum and Dave's relationship. I knew she was used to being controlled and that was the texture their relationship would always have.

'It's fine to go home, Mum,' I smiled. Dave would not ruin my day, no one would because I was so full of joy.

I had been extremely happy living with Kevin but now we were married I was even more so. I decided to keep my maiden name, not meaning Kevin any disrespect but just because it felt important to me to retain something of my own, a safety net. I was a wife again, but this time a cherished and respected wife. And that felt wonderful.

Angie looked after Owen so Kevin and I could have a few days' honeymooning in Skegness. It was there, on the beach, we scattered some of Bret and Brad Lee's ashes. Some of their ashes were buried in the Garden of Remembrance at the crematorium, but I had kept some because I knew that one day I'd find the right time and place to leave them somewhere special. There was no wind, not even the slightest whispering draught. But as soon as we stood on the shore and emptied the tiny urns a gust blew them straight back on to us. We were covered. Maybe my boys didn't want to leave us? They need never worry – they are with me always.

Every day in Skegness, Kevin and I walked past a gypsy lady, who was dressed in the stereotypical way of a headscarf and big earrings and whose green caravan bore a sign advertising palm readings. Whenever we saw her I deliberately avoided eye contact. I was so burnt by Geraldine's reading all those years ago that I had an aversion to anyone claiming to have insight into the future or spirit world.

On our last day, I stole a glance at her and she stared me straight in the eye and beckoned me towards her. I shook my head to say no, but Kevin gave me a soft nudge and said, 'Come on, let's speak to her – just for a laugh.' Reluctantly, I agreed.

The lady ushered us round to the back of her caravan and invited us to sit on her patio chairs. Warm and friendly, she quickly made us feel at ease despite my trepidation. And when she started to speak I felt relieved that nothing she said hit a chord. She said Kevin would have health issues with one side of the lower part of his body, which was ridiculous because he was perfectly well and had no health complaints whatsoever. And then she said something that made Kevin and I crease up with laughter.

'I hear the patter of tiny feet,' she said.

'No way!' I said. Kevin and I were using contraception and had no plans to add to our new little family.

But the gypsy shook her head confidently and was insistent. 'I definitely see a new arrival for you. And it's a girl.'

That was confirmation that we were hearing a load of nonsense. Everyone knew there was no way I could carry a girl. The gypsy finished off her reading by telling us we would, in time, move into a bigger white house, but Kevin and I didn't intend moving from his home. So after half an hour of silliness we bade her a friendly goodbye and left a £10 note, which we wrote off as payment for a bit of fun.

Married life has been as happy as we hoped but of course we have our ups and downs. Our relationship stays steady and strong, but sometimes luck can knock us back a bit. Celebrating the New Year of 2006 had a disastrous end because Kevin slipped on the dance floor of the club and could not get up. He'd had hardly anything to drink because we'd brought his mum out with us to see in the bells but he fell awkwardly and broke his leg in three places. He had it in a full-length cast for nine months and in that time I became the main breadwinner. I went out to work and he stayed home with Owen but it didn't feel at all as it had with Steve. I would never have let that happen, nor would Kevin. But now we worked around Kevin's injury as best we could and I would never complain about working hard. It seemed the gypsy was right about only one of her predictions about Kevin's health but we knew that was just a coincidence.

After the low of Kevin's accident we enjoyed a beautiful high. A course of antibiotics brought relief from my nasty chest infection but also interfered with my Pill, which resulted in a wonderful surprise.

Our daughter, Katie Marie, came into the world on 23 October 2006. At the scan, I tearfully asked again and again if the sonographer would confirm our baby was a girl.

'It's impossible,' I said, wiping away the tears and too scared to believe something that seemed too good to be true.

'I am as positive as I possibly can be,' she smiled. 'You have a very healthy-looking baby girl.'

I'd always wanted a daughter but had grown to believe Steve when he said I couldn't carry girls because I was too evil. I cried with joy and sheer disbelief the first time I held her. She was a gorgeous little thing, really affectionate and petite.

Owen was immediately besotted with her – we all were. At first I wondered how to play with a daughter because sons were all I'd known but I had a fabulous time buying her dolls and tea sets and playing with them together. I loved choosing frilly pink outfits and dressing her immaculately because I was giving her the childhood things I myself had never had. Now I had a darling little boy and girl with my loving husband and I felt truly blessed.

Sadly we lost one of the treasured children in our extended family in May 2009. Benjamin, my sister Nicky's son, died in his sleep, aged 13. He was such a special little boy, who always showed a happy, positive and loving spirit that defied the fact Hunter syndrome and other health complications since birth had put major physical obstacles in his way. His condition was degenerative so, although he was at one time able to walk and talk, his condition quickly went downhill. Towards the end of his life, poor Ben needed a special wheelchair and adapted bed to help ease the discomfort of his curved spine. He was a lovely-looking kid, with bright-blue eyes and spiky hair. Ben was truly adored and left a gaping hole in our family when he passed away.

Nicky brought Ben up single-handedly because her relationship with Ben's dad didn't last and she didn't tell anyone in her family his name. Devoted to him, she tirelessly cared for his every need. She was bereft when Heaven took him and my heart ached for her. I kissed Ben's hand and said goodbye when I went to see his pale lifeless body in bed and it was another traumatic time for us all. Unfortunately, because Ben was so young and died in his sleep, his passing was classed as an unexplained death so the police had to visit Mum's house to investigate. Ben's bedroom was treated as a crime scene and they questioned Nicky. We all had a horrible feeling of being held under suspicion, even though we knew it was normal police procedure. I hope I was able to somehow support Nicky throughout Ben's funeral, but I worry that I sobbed so much during the service that she ended up comforting me instead.

To try to further strengthen the family bond I spent every Saturday at Mum's house with the kids. She and I had grown closer than ever and enjoyed really good, open and honest chats together but I couldn't really say the same about Dave and me. One Saturday, as Owen and Katie played on the sitting-room floor, some sport came on TV and Dave shouted at them to be quiet. My conversation with Mum stopped mid-flow.

'Right, kids – get your coats on and let's go home. We're going home right now.'

Mum looked alarmed. 'What? Dee, don't go. Don't walk out. Why are you leaving all of a sudden?'

'No one, but NO ONE, ever shouts at my kids,' I said, 'especially not HIM!'

Dave looked mortified as I stormed past him to the front door but I would not tolerate any aggression towards my children. I would not stand by and let my little ones experience even the tiniest flash of my harsh history. As I strapped them into their car seats, I could hear Mum in the house, having a go at Dave: 'Now look what you've done! After everything Dee's been through, you've upset her again.'

I could tolerate Dave but only up to a point. And if he pushed me over it or even gave a slightest hint of any kind of threatening behaviour, then he would know about it. There was no way on earth I'd let Dave walk all over me, no way my hardened attitude towards him would soften. Not even when he received his cancer diagnosis.

Chapter 28

Losing A Stepdad; Gaining A Mother

In the early days of Dave's throat cancer, which was diagnosed in March 2009, Mum looked after him at home but after a few weeks he deteriorated to the point where he couldn't recognise people and wouldn't talk to Mum so was admitted to hospital. He caught pneumonia there and never came home.

It was odd that in his last days he met even those closest to him with a blank expression as if they were strangers. And for someone who had been so vocal throughout his life it was weird to see him with precious little to say. But one thing he did say, over and over again, was: 'When is Dee coming to pick me up?' I will never know if he kept saying it just because I was the only driver in the family and that was the last piece of random knowledge his senile mind surrendered. Sometimes I think there was a deeper reason than that. I was the person Dave was harshest to throughout his life and it seems ironic that I would be the last one he would know in his dying days. Did guilt play on his conscience until the very end?

He never once said sorry for his bully-boy ways throughout my upbringing.

The evening before Dave died, I visited him in hospital. As I looked at him, frail, grey-skinned and old in his hospital bed surrounded by machines and tubes, I realised that life has a way of biting cruel people on the backside. As I sat at the bottom of his bed, I said, 'You're not looking so tough now, are you, Dave?'

Had I forgiven him for the brutal way he treated my elder sisters and me? Yes, for Mum's sake and because after everything I'd gone through with Steve there was no room for any grudges or hatred in my heart. But would I forget it? No way!

When Mum and Nicky came to the hospital to spend time with Dave, I said my last 'ta-ra' to him. I didn't look back at him as I walked out the door. Mum and Nicky left at 3am and got a taxi home, but at 4am the nurses phoned them and said, 'Come back, Dave hasn't got long.' Mum and Nicky rang Angie and they all got another taxi back to the hospital to be with Dave in his final moments.

That night, I purposely did not take my phone into the bedroom. I was not prepared to drive through the night to sit up for hours with someone who had treated me the way he had. When I woke the next day and saw 16 missed calls on my phone, I turned to Kevin and said, 'Dave's died.' I didn't feel sad.

There was a good turnout at Dave's funeral, which took place six months after Ben's. All his fishing friends turned up and eulogised the legendary Dave Angel, who would always share out his competition prize money by buying everyone drinks at the bar. But they didn't really know him. They didn't know that he was splurging the family income on alcohol while his young stepdaughters were Sellotaped into their bedrooms, rarely adequately dressed or fed and frequently beaten.

Dave's death didn't hurt me: you can't be forced to love someone even when they've died. So I didn't cry at his funeral. Nor did Mum. I felt really sorry for her and was surprised by her lack of tears. I always thought Mum must have really loved Dave because she seemed to prioritise him over her young kids.

'I know why I'm not crying, but what about you, Mum?' I said after the funeral service.

'I just can't cry,' she told me. 'And I don't even know why.'

It wasn't true love or even blind love that kept Mum with Dave for over 30 years. All she had ever known was to be mentally and physically controlled and beaten down. She was scared of Dave and grew used to his ways. And I bear her no resentment for that because I know what it's like to be trapped with a man so manipulative and abusive that you are too fearful to even think your own thoughts. No apologies were needed from Mum because Dave's wrongs did not represent her. I don't think there are many mums who can honestly say they have never made mistakes when it comes to their children. I know I certainly have.

I try to look for the positives in every situation, even my childhood at the mercy of Dave. When I scratch around for something good to say about him, I think his too-tough ways made me headstrong and gave me the high tolerance levels I needed to get me through the Steve years. Maybe he gave me the iron will that served me well and kept me standing in later life.

Mum truly blossomed after Dave's death. She really came out of her shell and became much more extrovert, more adventurous and way more fun. She and Dave had never been on a foreign holiday together but after he died she saved throughout the year for a trip to Benidorm and enjoyed every minute there. She took computer classes and is now a whizz on the internet; she even learned to ride a bicycle and looks like a kid zooming around the streets on it with a big grin on her face. These days, she laughs more and cries less because she doesn't fear anyone. As a child I remembered seeing Mum change for the better whenever Dave went on his annual fishing trip to Denmark and now that change is permanent.

I have never had a conversation with Mum about the harsh realities of my childhood – I have never felt the need. Mum is now devoted to all her grandkids and does everything she can to help me and my sisters. With no one to boss her around or abuse her, she is now the mother she always should, and could, have been.

Mum is particularly close to Grace Ivy, maybe because she was there in the labour ward when she was born to Kevin and me on 14 June 2010. Just as I had been with Katie, I was on the Pill when I fell pregnant with Grace. I like to imagine both my daughters were really determined to be here. Maybe they really wanted me to be their mummy after a very bad man told me I would never have girls. Maybe my little girls wanted to prove a grown man wrong.

Kevin, our three kids and I live in a two-bedroom council house that's small but well-kept. My children have been brought up without much money but with an abundance of love.

Grace is hilarious. She's a very outgoing, comedic little thing. My mum loves cuddling her and saying, 'Come here, you cheeky little monkey – I don't half love you, you know.' I tell my kids I love them numerous times a day. Life is so short that whatever they do, wherever they go or whatever happens to them I want them to have a fresh memory of me saying, 'I love you, forever and always.'

Katie is our little drama queen. She sees a tiny spider as a tarantula, a stream as a huge lake and is scared of her own shadow, whereas Grace couldn't give a stuff. A deep thinker, Katie often drifts off into her own dreamy world but is also prone to diva outbursts. Kevin says she gets her stroppiness from me but what she's definitely inherited from him is her beautiful singing voice. Without ever having any lessons, her voice has vibrato and power that gives it an almost operatic tone. So, although Katie's a little scaredy-cat, once she's behind a microphone and on stage she brims with confidence and doesn't so much as wobble under the pressure and scrutiny of a large audience. She has sung solo at school a good few times and had the parents in tears and the entire school on their feet during a long standing ovation. She has far less passion for school work.

Owen is a clever young man who loves computers and all sorts of gadgets. He's a happy-go-lucky lad and has been a good boy ever since he was a baby but he is also a very sensitive soul and gets upset easily. I have a feeling Owen will always look after his old mum.

Often, when I look at Owen, I have to catch my breath for a few seconds. With his big brown eyes, shy smile and wavy dark hair, he looks so much like Bret and Brad Lee that I sometimes have to stop myself calling him their names. Once he reached the age of nine, I felt a plethora of emotions. I was daunted by the thought of raising a nine-year-old boy because I'd never had a child who lived to that age, so how would I cope? At the same time I was relieved that he'd got that far because in my mind my sons only lived until they reached the age of eight.

I still feel like a mum of five. Bret and Brad Lee's pictures are all over my house and Owen, Katie and Grace ask about their other brothers all the time. We all go to their headstone at the Garden of Peace at the crematorium every weekend and leave three flowers, one for each of my boys and one for the little girl lost before she lived. I have four of Bret and Brad Lee's favourite teddy bears and always leave two there so I can take the other pair home to wash away week's worth of weather. Their headstone is engraved with intertwined letter Bs and inscribed with: 'Together forever, taken from me in February

2002. I will be with you again soon, love Mummy'. Owen, Katie and Grace don't know that I also go to the crematorium a lot during the week when they're at school because it's quieter and better.

Kevin and I don't hide from our children the fact that Bret and Brad Lee lived but we are gentle with the truth about how they died. Grace says her biggest brothers are 'with Jesus' and then adds the names of the family dogs we lost to the Heaven roll call. We believe honesty is the best policy with the kids because, although we did it with the best intentions, at first we lied to Owen about Bret and Brad Lee's deaths and that seriously backfired.

Owen found one of the newspaper stories I'd done in the past and learned the brutal truth about his elder brothers' deaths from cold, hard newsprint.

'Mummy, you lied to me,' he said.

'Sorry, son?'

'You said Bret and Brad Lee were very poorly and that's why they're in Heaven. But they weren't poorly. They were killed by their daddy, weren't they?'

I was well and truly caught off-guard and it was a sore lesson to me never to lie to my children. So Owen and I sat down with photos of Bret and Brad Lee and I tried to explain as softly as I could stark facts too horrible for any young child's ears. Owen sat quietly and tearfully when he heard my story of how his lovely big brothers were taken by a daddy who was very nasty and definitely not anything like Kevin. He didn't need to hear the gory details – no one does. I wish I didn't know them myself.

'I am so sorry for not telling you the truth, Owen. Mummy was trying to look after you and look out for you. The truth isn't nice and I tried to shield you from that.'

'They might be dead, but they're still my brothers,' said Owen. 'Do you think their daddy will come for me, Katie or Grace?'

Owen asked for reassurances, over and over again, that Bret and Brad Lee's bad daddy was dead.

'He is dead and buried, son,' I said. 'He will never come here, he will never hurt you or anyone ever again. Mummy and Daddy will always look after you and protect you. And now that Bret and Brad Lee are in Heaven, nothing can hurt them ever again either.'

'I understand, Mummy,' said Owen, giving me a tight hug. And while Owen and I held each other tightly during that hug I really felt as if Bret and Brad Lee were standing beside us, smiling and saying, 'See, Mum, we told you everything would be OK.'

Chapter 29

*Happy To Be
A Working Mum*

All my life I considered people who work in an office to be incredibly glamorous, successful and mystifying because I had no earthly idea what they did at a desk all day. I understood jobs that involved carrying a mop, wearing a cook's pinny or cleaning bathrooms but not shuffling papers and tapping away on a computer. I never dreamt I would ever become one of those office workers. So, when Gemma got a managerial job in an insurance office and suggested I applied to be an administrative assistant there, I thought, 'Those jobs don't go to women like me.'

But I got it. I was thrilled to know I would actually become a white-collar worker. On my first day when I stepped into the office that shone with chrome and glass and was lined with rows of smartly dressed people concentrating hard on their computer screens, I felt out of my depth. But I managed to keep my nerve, was well trained on the job and took meticulous notes about everything I have to do so I never forget a single task. For the last two years I have worked four days a week in that insurance office, checking people's identification documents and making sure they have all the correct documentation to make a claim. I am grateful to Gemma and everyone there who has given me a chance.

It took me a while to have the confidence to be myself with my colleagues. If anyone knew me as 'the woman whose husband killed her kids', no one said, and I was glad of that. Sometimes I have so much going on in my head that it's more peaceful and relaxing to come to work and concentrate on the job in hand rather than what's on my mind (which is always Bret and Brad Lee). But because of my need to warn other women about the dangers of abusive relationships I always agree to be interviewed if ever the media request it. Whenever another despicable crime – which Americans call 'filicide' or 'family annihilation', which are horrible names for terrible deeds – takes place, I'm often called to speak to newspapers, magazines and TV stations to try to somehow explain how it feels to lose your children to their own father. I never refuse because I want to get the message out there, which is why I've been on ITV's *This Morning* three times now. Maybe I'm a spokeswoman for mothers whose children are killed in the worst way possible. Tragically, there are many other women in my position but they are probably too upset to talk about their husbands murdering their kids. I only feel able to do so because I'm still numb.

My job appraisal took place shortly after my last TV appearance, and my boss and I spent a good while talking about my lost sons rather than my work. He told me that he could not believe that the same woman he'd seen on television had been working for him for months. He said, 'My wife and I saw you on telly and we can't believe it's you. We Googled you and could not get our heads around what we read. How are you still living? How on earth do you manage to come into the office every day?'

I get up and out to work every day because I have to. Bret and Brad Lee are on my mind from the moment I wake up to those drowsy, mind-swirling minutes before I fall asleep. Sometimes grief bears down so heavily I fear I might not be able to get out of bed or face a new day, ever. But then I hear Grace, Katie and Owen downstairs while Kevin makes their breakfast and I'm reminded that my family needs me. I could sit in a corner and be an alcoholic bum, spending each day drinking myself into a state of oblivion but what good would I be to anyone then? If I was put on this earth to be a good mummy, then that's what I am going to be and I will let nothing stop me. I found a good man to love me unconditionally and I owe it to Kevin to be the best I can be. So each day I get out of bed, I kiss my three youngest children and husband goodbye and tell them I love them before setting off to work. And in the office where I feel proud to be every day, I do my work to the best of my ability.

The longer I've worked there, the more genuine friends I've made and the more comfortable I've felt about reminiscing about Bret and Brad Lee. I love talking about Bret and Brad

Lee because it keeps them alive. I'm not going to airbrush them out of my mind or my conversations because something horrific happened to them. They are never far from my thoughts. Instead, I tell people I had five children but my eldest two are passed. People then understand why I am sometimes quiet or look as if I have the weight of the world on my shoulders, but they might not understand that, although I smile on the outside, if you cut me open you'd see that a lot of my insides are dead.

I always plunge into a deep low at the turn of each New Year because it hits me hard that I'm facing another year without my eldest boys. Kevin, my mum and my sisters worry themselves sick and urge me to go to the doctors to see about getting counselling but I've still never done it and I still resist anti-depressants. I'm still scared to let go and admit that I haven't really grieved. After the boys' anniversaries in February, I usually start picking myself up again.

People say time is a healer. Is it heck. Whenever I visit their headstone at the crematorium I still cry as much as I did in those early days of losing Bret and Brad Lee. Time has served only to age and fade the memories of their voices, the feeling of their soft skin and the warm cuddles. That makes my grief harder to bear. Deep down I still feel as hurt and as raw as I did at the Howard Johnson Hotel on the first night without my boys. I still feel in shock and each time I see boys' clothes in ASDA and think, 'That would look lovely on Bret and Brad Lee', I have to jolt myself back to the reality that they are not here. But in the hurly-burly of daily domestic life there is little time to dwell. I make sure of that.

Every day I struggle desperately with the burden of guilt. Not just guilt about leaving Bret and Brad Lee that night back in February 2002, but at the thought that I don't do enough for Owen, Katie and Grace. When Owen or Katie look through pictures of Bret and Brad Lee, they sometimes say, 'They were on holiday a lot – why don't we ever go on holiday like them?' The money from my insurance office job is respectably earned and carefully budgeted, but is rarely enough for even the simplest of luxuries. In fact, whenever Kevin and I have been hit with an unexpected bill we've had to pawn some of our belongings. Most material things mean little to me and I don't miss them but I do wish I hadn't had to pawn the gold locket that held pictures of Bret and Brad Lee close to my chest on my wedding day. I deeply regret the fact Kevin and I have had to pawn our original wedding bands. By the time we had the cash to buy our jewellery back, it was too late and the locket and rings had been sold on. It was upsetting and I bemoaned the fact our finances are so scarce over a tearful cup of tea with my husband, but before I'd even finished that cuppa I'd cheered up by reminding myself that money matters little and the health and happiness of my children matters a lot. To me items of jewellery are just life's baubles but children are the building blocks.

This year, I was taken on part-time at the local chip shop, where I clock up 10 hours a week during evenings and weekends out with my nine-to-five work in the insurance office. That's because I have promised the kids that we will have our first family holiday together and we hope to go to Skegness. I will graft every hour I can until we have enough money for that holiday.

It's hard for Kevin to find work because of his leg injury, so, while I work, he stays at home with the children. It's an arrangement that works well for our family because I am so cautious about whom I leave with my kids. I am too scared to leave them with anyone I don't trust implicitly. But I have never been scared of hard work.

In fact, other than the welfare of my family, I'm not scared of anything now. I will let no one push me around, no one intimidate me. If ever I see a man arguing with a woman, I watch silently from a distance in case he does anything aggressive to her. If he dared lift a hand I wouldn't hesitate to approach him. And if anyone has a go at me I stand my ground and never get riled because I think, 'I have faced bigger bullies than you'll ever be'. I have endured my greatest fear, which was losing my kids, and I have survived. Once you've reached rock bottom there is only one way to go, and that's to bounce back. In my situation, I had to choose to sink or swim. And I chose to swim.

Friends and family buoy me up. I suspect there is a secret network of people close to me who call each other when they are worried about me and they all look out for me. I don't tell them often enough how much I appreciate that. Family is more important to me than ever now, because I know how much it can hurt when they go. Kevin and I have just put a deposit on a new house, which is much bigger than the one we've been in since 2002. It's next door to Mum on one side and my sister Amy on the other. When I sneaked down the stairs to leave home at the age of 16, I never thought one day I would be excited to move right next door. It's funny how life can take us full circle.

Amanda emigrated to Australia five years ago and I miss her terribly. We kept in touch by letter for a long time while she was out there, but I lost her address just before she moved house. I would love to hear from her again; I would be thrilled if she read the book and realised just how much I appreciate her and got in touch again. But maybe now, as she works for an Australian police force, it's someone else's turn to have Amanda's time and selfless support. If she could help me get through what I did, she could help anyone in the darkest, direst of circumstances. Only a very exceptional person could do that.

Gemma has another lovely little girl now and, for the last two years, she and Loren have been in contact with Konrad. Loren had been asking to see her dad for a while and Gemma eventually relented and contacted him through Facebook. Even though Konrad did not see Loren for 14 years and there was a sense of awkwardness when they first met two years ago at Sutton Park, they have already managed to form a good relationship.

Gemma says Konrad is a very different man now and they get on well, which is good for Loren's sake and great if it helps further heal Gemma's scars from the past. She and Konrad have both been engaged but never remarried. Incredibly, they have never divorced. Konrad even calls round to Gemma's house to fix her car and bits and bobs around the place. She would like Konrad and I to talk more but, much as I'd like to bury the hatchet, I don't think I'm ready yet. Maybe I'm still too sore. I haven't heard a word nor seen sight of Stacey in years. Gemma's mum and nan both died in 2005. It's a shame they didn't see that, despite the odds stacked against them, Gemma and Konrad's relationship worked out OK in the end.

And me? If you see me on the street and ask how I'm doing, I'll tell you I'm fine. I'm permanently busy and thoroughly exhausted, but isn't every mother? I wish I could relax more about letting my kids roam free, but maybe inevitably I'm an over-protective mum. I'm the mother you see at soft play areas, helicoptering above their child in case so much as a sponge ball hits them. Owen will start high school soon and has never been allowed to play in the street on his own, never been allowed a sleepover. When he went on a school trip last year, I was on tenterhooks for weeks beforehand, stressed to the hilt while he was away and mightily relieved when he came home. I am far too much of a worrier for his liking and I leap to his defence so often he finds me embarrassing. At his football practice recently, another young lad said, 'Don't be stupid, Owen,' and I couldn't help myself.

'Don't you *ever* call my son stupid!' I told the kid, who now looked wide-eyed to be confronted about a throwaway comment by a fuming mother.

Owen was aghast. 'Leave it, Mum, please.'

'No! Who does he think he is, calling you stupid?'

I wish I wasn't so short-fused and over-the-top about protecting and defending my children but I think that's another one of the lasting legacies of what Steve did. I hope my kids will one day understand why I have to be so eagle-eyed when they are around. Maybe they won't fully grasp it until they have children of their own and enjoy that all-encompassing love that all parents feel for their little ones. All good parents, anyway.

Chapter 30
Closure From Beyond

The late evening phone call from Gemma in November 2013 really unnerved me.

'Dee, I have been to a psychic and I've got something to tell you.' She sounded pretty anxious.

'What is it, Gemma? Are you all right? Is it something about my boys?'

'Sorry, Dee – I don't want to tell you over the phone. Can we meet for a chat tomorrow?'

Gemma's call made my mind race with so many questions I didn't sleep that night. We met at Angie's house so I had family around when I heard the news that would send me into a tailspin of despair.

Gemma said, 'Dee, I went to see a lady called Pat, who is psychic, last night. She was amazing. She told me my mum and nan came through and gave me messages from them that she couldn't possibly have known.

'But Pat kept interrupting Mum and Nan's messages by saying, "Hold on, there's a little boy desperately trying to get through.

His name begins with B." Eventually, she said, "The little boy has come to the front now. He says his name is Br... Br... maybe Braden? Or Brendan? He says please can you tell their mummy they are OK. Please tell her not to worry about them.'"

Gemma was in tears as she told me. And I was so stunned I didn't speak, or even breathe. I had always been sceptical of people who claimed contact with the spirit world but the message from a lady Gemma and I had never met before was heart-stoppingly specific. I know the message was intended as a comfort but I was distraught.

'Why did only one of my boys come through, Gemma?' I said, with tears and anxiety welling. 'They were always together. Always. If one was invited to a party and the other one wasn't, the first one wouldn't go. They were rarely out of each other's sights. Even on their headstone it says "together forever". Why aren't they together now?'

I wanted an answer no one on this earth could give. My over-tired and emotionally wrung-out mind started torturing itself. Did only one of my boys come through to the psychic because Steve had dragged one of my sons down to Hell with him? Why else would they ever be apart? It troubled me so much over the next few days that I began to feel ill, could not concentrate at work and became distant, preoccupied, snappy and weepy at home.

There was only one way to ease my turmoil and that was to visit psychic Pat myself. Despite the accuracy of the palm-reading gypsy in Skegness during my honeymoon, I was still suspicious and intended seeing Pat to chastise her for conveying a message that had caused me a huge amount of upset.

Claire, my good friend at work, said she'd come with me. She was selfless to volunteer because she is scared witless of anything in any way 'spooky'. I asked her to book our appointment for 6 February – the boys' anniversary.

'Let's see if she picks up that date – then we'll know how good she is,' I told Claire.

The night before our appointment I didn't sleep a wink. I kept reliving events of the boys' anniversary, wishing I could go back in time and take them safely out of Steve's vice-like grip. One minute I convinced myself that everything Pat told Gemma was just a wild coincidence and the skill of a charlatan, definitely not a gift from a medium. The next minute I felt wholly convinced everything she said really was from the heavenly world because how else could she know so much? That left the most agonising question of all: why weren't my sons together?

Katie had real trouble sleeping that night, too. She must have had a terrible nightmare because she woke with an ear-shattering scream in the early hours, her eyes saucer-sized with fear, and I had to stay with her for an hour until she calmed down and drifted off.

The weather on 6 February 2014 was so cold, windy and rainy that the radio weather forecaster suggested people stayed home and didn't make unnecessary journeys. But there was no way I would miss psychic Pat's appointment because I was in turmoil at why only one of my inseparable sons seemed to want to communicate with her. I drove Claire to her house in Tamworth in my Renault Espace, which has seven seats, and tried to make light of the situation by joking that we needed the extra room for all the ghosts we were taking along with us.

'Stop it, Dee!' Claire said, shuddering.

When we got to Pat's house she opened the door and said, 'Well, I see you've brought a lot of spirits with you tonight.' Claire looked like she might bolt. Soon the joking stopped.

Pat, a well-presented petite lady in her sixties, didn't make eye contact with either of us at first. She only looked straight at me, almost through me, when she sat opposite me on one of two little sofas in a rather plain room upstairs, which had just a coffee table, low-level lamp and a rug over floorboards. When the light flickered for a second, I smiled to myself that maybe Trish wanted to have a word with me but within minutes the atmosphere became more serious as Pat began delivering messages from late family members with a precision I found hard to question.

'I have a man here called Mick. He's asking you to please tell his wife and daughter that he is OK and is always with them.'

My sister Angie's partner, who is her little girl's father, had passed away 21 years ago but was called Mick.

Then Pat fell silent for a while and I worried she would be unable to deliver any message from Bret or Brad Lee. Maybe it had all been a big waste of time. Maybe I should just leave my boys to rest in peace.

Then, looking not at me but into the near distance, she said, 'Sorry, what did you say? Brendan? Bret! Hang on – there's someone else with you. Braden? Who are you laughing at? You're a cheeky little boy for laughing at me just for getting your name wrong. You're telling me your name is Brad Lee?'

I burst into tears. Pat looked at me then and said, 'Why are you crying? These are your sons, aren't they? They're saying, "Please don't cry, Mum," and they're hugging you right now. I wish I could take a family photo now because you'd see they're right next to you and giving you a lovely warm embrace. They're calling it a double cuddle.'

I wanted to jump into Pat's body then so I could see exactly what she could see. And I do believe she could see or at least sense something from another world. Because using a phrase like 'double cuddle' was one the boys often said but one that I hadn't mentioned or heard in years.

If that was all Pat could tell me I'd have gone home feeling happy at just that tiny moment of love from my boys but she had even more jaw-dropping messages to pass on from them. She said, 'The boys are asking you why you bought two new wedding rings recently. They say there was no need because they know how much you and your new husband love each other, regardless.'

The previous day, Kevin and I had been to a second-hand jeweller's shop to buy new wedding bands. We had told no one because we were embarrassed at having to pawn our old ones.

'The boys say thank you for bringing three flowers to the crematorium for their anniversary earlier today. They said their little sister liked her flower too. She's here with them and she has the palest skin and the darkest hair. She's a beautiful little thing, she looks like Snow White.'

My eyes streamed with tears and my chest heaved with sobs.

'They also said thank you for planning to take everyone on holiday this year because you haven't been away since after the wedding. And they want me to tell you they are with you wherever you go.

'I have had to stop their father trying to come through today. The boys say their daddy is not going to ruin anything for them now. He's not going to hurt you, or them, ever again. Hold on, they're trying to tell me something. I've asked them how they died and they said, "Daddy took us for a ride in the car." Good God, they did have a horrible death. He killed them, didn't he?'

I nodded, my emotions now out of control and my heart rate off the scale.

Pat continued, 'The boys say that you must stop saying it was your fault. It was Daddy's fault. They say you mustn't blame yourself for anything because it would have happened whether you'd stayed or not. So you have to stop thinking like that because it's driving you mad. They're telling me that if you hadn't left he'd have killed you all and then they wouldn't have their new little brother and sisters. They want me to tell you they love their new brother and two sisters and promise to look after them always. Two of the three of them will go to university. They say their first little sister is a lovely singer. And they say the littlest sister is drop-dead gorgeous.

'Whenever you look at your other son they stand in front of him just so you can see them too. And they want me to tell you they are with you 24 hours a day and never leave you. They're saying, "We love you, Mummy, we do. Best friends forever."'

Throughout that utterly astounding time with psychic Pat, I nodded, cried, smiled and most of all ached for my boys. And towards the end she said something that made me gasp.

'The boys said they are sorry they woke their sister up last night. The covers fell off her bed and she was cold, so they picked them up and covered her up again. They said they didn't mean to wake her up or freak her out.'

Pat had given me the most incredible hour and 15 minutes of my life and wanted only £15 for it. She said she didn't do readings for a living but did them just because she started hearing things. If you ask me, she is truly gifted. Claire would agree, because she came downstairs after her reading with her mind blown by the spot-on personal and private messages from her late relatives. As Pat bid us goodbye, she said, 'See you again in two years.'

Claire and I stood outside Pat's house in the pouring rain, gobsmacked and trying to digest everything we'd just been told. I smoked two of Claire's cigarettes and these days I don't even smoke.

Kevin could not believe what he heard when I got home and breathlessly tried to relay all of the boys' messages through my tears and shrieks of amazement.

'I'm just glad you feel better, Dee. You even look better.'

That night, with Kevin's arms around me as usual, I slept better than I had done in years. The next day at work, colleagues commented about a new colour in my cheeks, shine in my eyes and a glow on my skin. Ever since Bret and Brad Lee died, I've desperately wanted to know if they were OK, if they were together, if they were looking after each other and if they knew I loved them. Hearing assurances of all of that, thanks to Pat, gave me more closure and comfort than years of counselling.

Chapter 31
Light At The End Of The Longest, Darkest Tunnel

Bret and Brad Lee would be, *should* be, fully grown men by now but I hope they wouldn't be too embarrassed to cuddle their old mum. I'd give anything just to hold them, just to touch their warm skin.

I imagine we would still be as close as ever; I know our bond would never have changed but our roles might have. In their late teens and early twenties, I think my boys would have looked after me and been my protectors rather than the other way round. And in their own little way, they had always done that: they always helped lift me when I was in the depths of Steve's hell. They were my duo of rainbows when my days were darkened by black clouds.

I still have a heart. Kevin, Owen, Katie and Grace and the rest of my family make sure it's still there. But it isn't the same shape anymore. It has two huge chunks ripped out and it's dented by hard knocks, coloured by deep bruises and looks like a child's scribble, with all sorts of straggly bits hanging from it. It isn't just broken, it's shredded into millions of little pieces that somehow clump together and still work, still keep me standing.

Although I'm still here, my thoughts are always elsewhere. Just because I'm carrying on, it doesn't mean I have forgotten about Bret and Brad Lee even for a moment. I have been through shock and bereavement of the most hateful and torturous kind, but I also had eight years of precious moments with my boys that no one can steal from me. I try to concentrate on those treasured times, not the traumatic ones.

I have experienced every emotion there is. Guilt can weigh me down, anger can make my stomach seize into a tight ball of fury but loss is the hardest to bear. I dearly wish my two eldest boys didn't just smile at me from picture frames. I wish I could magic them here again.

I get lost in time whenever I go upstairs looking for paperwork but instead find boxes of pictures of Bret and Brad Lee. The photograph albums are untainted by pictures of Steve. I can be upstairs, sitting on the floor against my bed for hours, just smiling and crying at happy snaps of my handsome eldest boys, their paintings, school jotters, tiny handprints, first and last curls. After a while Owen will come up and join me, and then Katie will come and sit on the other side of me. And before long Grace will clamber on the bed behind me and ask a thousand questions about her big brothers who are lost from this life but never from my mind.

'Weren't your brothers just lovely, kids?' I ask. And they always respond with sad little nods of agreement then lean into me for a consolatory squeezy hug.

Pictures, mementoes and memories of Bret and Brad Lee are the only things that bring me comfort. When people meet me they never know what to say about my boys but when they have a nice story to tell about them I feel warm inside again, even if I've heard that story a dozen times. I just like to know that people haven't forgotten them.

Well-meaning folk say they understand how I must feel. But that's impossible. Because when your terrifying nightmare comes true, no one dares to empathise. When you lose your kids like I did, to the man whose warped paternal instinct made him kill rather than protect his children, it's too horrific to imagine. It's as if your brain puts the brakes on before it goes to a really bleak place. Steve's crime was unthinkable but I'm glad hardly anyone can share my true feelings and emotions – I wouldn't wish that on anyone.

Nothing in the world can make me feel whole again. And that makes Kevin sad because he fixes everything for his family but he can't fix me. I know only too well his feeling of helplessness because I wasn't there to save my boys when they needed me most. But I can try my best to save other kids like them and other mums like me. I can urge them to leave at the first sign of aggression or violence. I can remind them that going back to a violent partner for the sake of the children is the very move that will harm them.

My greatest ambition is to set up a support group for survivors of domestic fatalities. I don't have high-brow qualifications in psychology or counselling, but unfortunately I do have the experience to empathise with other bereaved mums when they feel they are the only ones in the world going through such desolation. I would love it if one day even a little good could come of something so horrifically bad.

Lessons have been learned from Bret and Brad's death, which might have gone some way to helping others already. Years after Steve did what he did, there was an investigation into the lack of intervention from government agencies in the run-up to my boys' murders. The report, which was leaked to my regional paper, *Express & Star*, criticised the police, social services and women's refuges for not doing enough to help prevent the tragedy.

It confirmed that a year before Bret and Brad Lee were killed I had warned police and refuge staff that Steve was capable of killing both himself and me. Sightings of me with bruising had been recorded, and on reading this I realised how naive I'd been to think that no one around me had known about the beatings I endured each week. Officials were aware and they were concerned, but the agencies didn't link up to class my boys as 'at risk'. The information was held in isolation and not pieced together to give the full picture and raise alarm bells.

I also learned about Steve's life before I met him. The report said his family first came to the attention of social services in relation to Konrad and Stacey. It stated that staff at Konrad's school reported verbal and physical aggression by Steve, which included throwing the deputy headteacher into the swimming pool. Steve roared laughing whenever he recounted that disgraceful deed.

After Bret and Brad Lee were born, social services noted concerns that Konrad was sleeping in a shed. And the catalogue of police call-outs and neighbour reports of domestic abuse in the early hours were all detailed in the report. The review panel said the incidents that involved knives should have been treated very seriously.

The report concluded that the issue of children's safety was lost because agencies concentrated on the adults. And it called for a raft of new policies to be introduced to guard against any other such tragedies. I hope they are working, I hope they are saving lives.

The findings and new preventative measures came far too late for me, of course. It was strange to read that so many officials had files on me and my boys yet we were totally unaware of that. I have always been grateful to everyone at the women's refuges, but I also see that more could be done. Maybe if I'd had follow-up calls I could have explained that my husband hadn't kept those promises about not hitting me. Maybe if my boys had been found new schools right away I'd have been less inclined to come back to the only home I'd known in adulthood.

But of course the blame does not lie with any agency. I was thoroughly brainwashed by Steve. He got into my head and I always returned home from the refuge, always dropped police charges. I did that for the sake of Bret and Brad Lee, not for Steve. But I did it out of fear of Steve.

I have to live with that for the rest of my life and have paid a huge price. I will never get over it but I am getting through it. I've counselled myself through the years without my sons and get stronger every year. It's a slow and agonising healing process and that's why it's taken me 12 years to put my life down on paper. That bashed-up, battle-scarred heart of mine is slowly knitting together but it will always have holes.

I know life can be cruel and short so I'm here to try to make it happy for my three youngest kids and my husband. And I'm getting there. I'm not superhuman and I often come close to cracking, but I'm a survivor, not a victim. Love from my family, and for my family, keeps me going. Love and life has taught me there is light at the end of each tunnel – even the longest, darkest one.

Chapter 32
Dearest Bret And Brad Lee

Writing my life story has been my therapy. I'm better with words when they're written rather than spoken. When people ask me how I am, I have to concentrate on painting on a smile. Usually, my answer is: 'I'm fine, thanks.' But when I write I can say much more and express my true feelings. That's a useful outlet because, really, I am far from fine.

There are many lovely people around me who would be perfectly happy to listen patiently and sympathetically to my innermost thoughts but I worry that hearing about my grief will exacerbate their own. My mum still can't talk about the grandsons she lost without crying so I don't want to fully offload or confide in her.

The people I really long to communicate with are Bret and Brad Lee. So, if ever I'm feeling churned up, whenever my feelings are bubbling under the surface and threaten to overspill, I find a quiet corner of the house and pour my feelings out in a letter to my two eldest sons. I don't know what a grief counsellor would say about my writing to the dead. Maybe it's bonkers but it makes me feel better. For a while anyway.

Dearest Bret and Brad Lee,

I am missing you both like mad. You probably already know that. You probably can see everything I do from up there in Heaven but I wanted to tell you anyway. We should always take the time to tell people nice things. I wonder if I told you I loved you enough times when you were here? I think it all the time now you are gone.

I hope you're OK up there. I wonder if you are spending time with your cousin Ben, who is another of God's special angels. And have you managed to find Granddad Dennis? I wish I knew what Heaven was like. If you have met God I hope you remembered your manners.

Thank you for sending me your messages through psychic Pat. I hope you didn't mind me talking to her. Lots of people say it's best to leave the dead to rest in peace but you two will never really be dead to me. You're always living in my mind, being as funny and cheeky as always.

It was good to hear from Pat that you'd seen the gifts we leave for you at the crematorium each week. Sometimes when I'm washing your old teddies I think back to all the treats you loved so much. It made me smile when I remembered that whenever you had pocket money you wanted to spend it on microwave ready meals rather than toys or sweets. You two had funny little quirks like that. You were like little old men. I wish you'd had the chance to become big men.

Lots of people visit your headstone and stop for a while to think about you. Your school friends and teachers will never forget you and wonder, like I do, if you'd have grown up to become footballers. Or maybe you'd have become pop stars. I'd love to hear you two sing karaoke with your little sister Katie. I wonder, do you hear us up in heaven? Owen has inherited your great football skills – do you play up there? And Grace, I bet she makes you two laugh when you're watching over her.

No one visits Daddy's grave. No one can believe what he did to you, even now. I am so sorry, boys. I always said I would be here for you always but now I am here and you are not. I wish I'd taken you both with me when I ran away from Daddy. I wish he'd taken me instead of you. I hope you can forgive me. I wish, as we always promised, we could be best friends forever.

In my daydreams I try to imagine what you look like now. Psychic Pat says children still grow in Heaven but they stop aging when they get to 21. These days the police use computer images to work out what children who have been missing for years probably look like now. One day I'm going to ask them to make a picture of you two like that. I know for sure you will still be handsome – you two always were.

I better go because it's tea-time and your brother and sisters will be hungry by now. Just like you, they call florets of broccoli mini trees and think peas are silly because they never stay on the fork. They are so similar to you in so many ways. I love them with everything I have and I know you would too. But Bret and Brad Lee, no one will ever replace you. You will always be Mummy's little angels and I will never forget you. I will miss you forever and I will love you to infinity.

Be good boys.

Lots of love, until I see you again, Mummy xx

A Final Note

I have spoken out and bared my soul in the hope that I can help others escape abusive relationships before it is too late.

If you read my story and think it's so extreme or so rare it couldn't possibly happen to you or anyone you know, sadly, statistics show otherwise. According to an NSPCC report on child homicide statistics in March 2014, based on a five-year average, one child is killed at the hands of their parent every 10 days in England and Wales. Ever since my boys died at their father's hands, I have felt guilty about every life lost.

This list is not exhaustive because many more cases are unreported in the media but, since the day Steve killed my boys, these are some of the children taken by the people they trusted most. And to them all, I would like to say sorry.

14 July 2002

Claude Mubiangata doused himself in petrol and set it alight as he sat in his car with his four children: Alpha, 12, Cindy, nine, Chriony, seven, and Aaron, three. They were found in the burnt-out car in North Woolwich, London. An inquest heard that Mubiangata carried out his actions because his wife Chantalle refused to give him custody of the children. Chantalle said she only let her estranged husband take them out because she could not believe anyone would harm their own offspring.

1 February 2004

Doctor Jayaprakash Chiti, from Ipswich, Suffolk, murdered his wife, Dr Anupama Damera, before taking his own life and that of their two-year-old son, Pranau, by holding him and plunging 160ft from a bridge. He was jealous of his wife's professional success as a breast cancer surgeon.

29 November 2005

Hospital radiographer Gavin Hall, 33, killed his three-year-old daughter Amelia at their Northamptonshire home when he discovered his wife's affair with a judge. He fed Amelia, known as Millie, anti-depressant pills to make her drowsy before smothering her with a rag soaked in chloroform then strangled her as she lay dying from the effects of the chemical. Hall was convicted of murder at Northampton Crown Court.

31 August 2006

Robert Tamar, a 48-year-old former paratrooper, stabbed his 15-month-old son Nathan to death and then killed himself after the child's mother failed to turn up on time to collect him from an access visit. Tamar attacked his ex-partner, Rachel Jones, 40, with a hammer outside their home in Winchester, Hampshire, before snatching their son. Rachel had left Tamar after a 12-year relationship because he had begun drinking heavily.

23 September 2007

Four-year-old Ryan Hawkins was stabbed to death by his dad Christopher at his home in Slaithwaite, near Huddersfield. His 13-year-old sister Donna was knifed 13 times by her father but survived. Hawkins had been violent and abusive towards his wife Valerie, 41, and killed their son in an act of revenge for leaving him and starting a new relationship. He was jailed for life.

15 June 2008

On Father's Day, Brian Philcox, 53, from Runcorn in Cheshire, drove his children, Amy, seven, and three-year-old Owen, in his Land Rover to a remote beauty spot in Snowdonia, North Wales, and sedated them with drugs and chloroform masks. He climbed into the back seat with them as exhaust fumes filled the car. All three died. Philcox had split from his wife, Lyn, 37, over his violent and controlling personality. He sent her a text telling her to enter his house. An envelope with the word 'Bitch' written on it was found glued to a kitchen worktop. Police later discovered that the act of ripping it off was supposed to spark an explosion from elaborate devices Philcox had hidden in his walls, skirting boards and under the kitchen table. They failed to go off.

2 August 2009

Gary Fisher, 48, from Solihull, murdered his teenage daughter, Chanelle Sasha Jones, as she sat in the passenger seat of his car. Fisher then drove around West Wales with the blood-soaked corpse of the 17-year-old for 10 hours until he was stopped by police. He claimed her killing was part of a suicide pact, a defence dismissed as 'idiotic' in court. In 2010, he was jailed and ordered to serve a minimum 20-year term.

20 August 2010

Chris Hall, 52, killed his six-year-old son and then himself with a lethal drugs cocktail in his home in Dorset, Poole. He had snatched the boy from his ex-partner, Rachel Wild, 35, and chillingly told her, 'I will take him to a place where you will never see him again.' Hall had feared he was about to lose his son, also called Chris, in a custody battle after Rachel left him and started a relationship with another man.

6 June 2011

David Oakes, 50, subjected his ex-partner Christine Chambers, 38, to an horrific sexual assault over three hours before he shot her at point-blank range three times and then shot their two-year-old daughter Shania. Oakes then attempted to shoot himself but survived. Four months into his life sentence, he died of cancer.

30 September 2012

Ex-Army sergeant and IRA bomb survivor Michael Pedersen, 51, from Surrey, fatally stabbed his children, Ben and Freya, aged six and seven, on an arranged visit with them after splitting from his wife, Erica, 43. He was described as 'controlling' and Erica had an injunction against him visiting the family home after he had broken her arm and shoulder. Pedersen took his own life by stabbing himself in the chest.

18 May 2013

Julian Stevenson, 48, used a kitchen knife to cut the throats of his children, Mathew, 10, and five-year-old Carla, in a fit of rage over a custody battle with his ex-wife. He had fled on a pair of roller skates but was found moments later, walking in the streets of the French city of Lyon, covered in blood. Stevenson is believed to have had a history of drinking and had his visitation rights curtailed after a violent clash with his ex-wife Stephanie in 2010. Months later in prison, he hanged himself.

12 February 2014

Greg Anderson, 54, stabbed and beat his 11-year-old son Luke to death with a cricket bat after a cricket training session in Melbourne, Australia. Luke's mum, Rosie Batty, 52, looked on in horror. Anderson was shot and killed by police. Warrants for Anderson's arrest on domestic violence and child pornography charges were active at the time of the attack.

Acknowledgements

To Kevin, thank you for loving me at my lowest and gently holding my hand to lead me back up again. You have proved to me that trust, kindness and love actually does exist. Thank you to my beautiful children, Owen, Katie and Grace, for somehow knowing how to make me laugh, even on my saddest days. Loving you four special people gives me a reason to live. You have made the impossible come true because my life is happy and bright again. Who ever thought I would feel that?

Mum, I hope you don't mind me talking about our early life and am so glad we have built bridges in later life. Being close to you now brings me great joy. Let's try not to cry so much about things in the past and together let's plan lots of laughs and fun times for our family's future.

To my sisters – Angie, Nicky, Sarah and Amy – we have all been through so much but each of us has learned that family comes first. Thanks for all the times you've propped me up. Let's always try to stick together.

I would never have got through what I did without Amanda Harvey. Thank you for being my rock at the worst time in my life and for telling me I could do it when I felt sure I couldn't. I admire, appreciate and miss you so much.

To Gemma, I wish we didn't have such a dark history but I am glad that you and I have each other now to help us through our recovery. You are one of the few people in the world who understands and I hope I am as supportive to you as you have been to me.

For all the volunteers I met at Women's Aid refuges. You gave me a safe place at the most dangerous times. It is my turn to help you now.

To the lady on the train, even though you are a relative stranger, you mean so much to me. You kept me going on that train journey to safety in Llandudno. Your letter warmed my black heart after the boys had died, and does each time I revisit the box of cards received after they were taken. How I wish I had never made my return journey.

Thank you to everyone, especially the children, who sent cards and letters after I lost my boys. I kept every single one and they comfort me whenever I'm feeling low.

West Midlands Police, I appreciate your investigations ensured that a man who could lie his way out of any situation was found guilty and died behind bars.

To Claire, thanks for coming to psychic Pat with me because I know you were secretly terrified but wanted to be by my side. And to Carol, for always listening to my good times and bad, and for brightening up my days with juicy gossip. I am honoured to have you two as friends.

Thank you to Sara Cywinski at Ebury for seeing the hope and inspiration of my story and for handling it with great care. While others called my book a psychological drama, you recognised that it is my real life.

One person who has played a major part in my life since 2005 is Julie McCaffrey. You are a wonderful, warm and caring person and have given me so much of your time, even though you are a mum to beautiful triplet girls. You have captured my life and voice perfectly. Your family must be very proud of you, I know I am.

Finally, and most importantly, to Bret and Brad Lee, thank you for being the most wonderful, loving sons I could ever have wished for. Thank you for the time we had together, and I am sorry that it was so short. I think of you, I miss you, every single day.